BUSINESS OBJECTIVES

Student's Book

Vicki Hollett

Recordarle a Fco q̆
enseñe Conversación telefónica

Oxford University Press

Contents

5 Reporting *page 40*

Objective	Topics	Language	Skills work
to report on past actions	Company history Saying when things happened Finding out what happened	Past simple tense Prepositions - time	*Reading:* products that didn't sell *Speaking:* reporting on a work project

6 Socializing *page 48*

Objective	Topics	Language	Skills work
to hold social conversations with business contacts	Business lunches Offering things Offering help Interests and routines Social chit-chat	Countable and uncountable nouns - *some* and *any* *Would you like ...?* *Shall I ...? / Let me ...* Expressions of frequency	*Speaking:* social conversations *Reading:* executive life-styles

7 Meetings *page 58*

Objective	Topics	Language	Skills work
to discuss corporate problems and decide what action to take	Recommending action Justifying decisions Making suggestions	*Should* Expressing opinions *Going to* (future)	*Listening:* a hotel's marketing policy *Speaking:* planning a new hotel

8 Making Arrangements *page 68*

Objective	Topics	Language	Skills work
to make and change arrangements	Timetables, plans, and arrangements Making appointments Invitations 1 Fixing a time Invitations 2	Present simple and continuous (future) *Would*	*Reading and Writing:* telex and email messages *Speaking:* arranging and re-arranging a schedule

9   Describing Trends   *page 78*

Objective	Topics	Language	Skills work
to describe and discuss figures and graphs	A balance sheet Describing changes Describing graphs Giving reasons	Prepositions - finance Verbs of change - *rise, fall, increase, decrease* Adjectives and adverbs Cause/effect connectors	*Writing:* divisional performance reports *Listening:* a country's economic performance *Speaking:* explaining a graph

10   Company Results   *page 88*

Objective	Topics	Language	Skills work
to discuss the recent performance and activities of a company	Giving news Targets Staffing levels	Present perfect simple tense	*Listening:* the radio business news *Speaking:* investment performance

11   Comparing Alternatives   *page 96*

Objective	Topics	Language	Skills work
to compare alternative courses of action	Comparing towns Comparing countries Comparing companies	Comparatives and superlatives *-er / more than ...* *...as...as* *the -est / the most ...*	Speaking: selecting a new site for a factory Reading: management styles

12   Planning Ahead   *page 108*

Objective	Topics	Language	Skills work
to discuss future work plans and schedules	Talking about quantity Predicting the future Giving advice	Countable and uncountable nouns - *much* and *many* *Will* - future facts and predictions *You'd better (not) ...*	*Listening:* a project briefing *Speaking:* planning a business venture

13 Business Travel *page 116*

Objective	Topics	Language	Skills work
to discuss changes to present arrangements	Air travel Rules and regulations Future possibilities	Modals of obligation *Mustn't* vs. *Don't have to* Open conditionals	*Speaking 1:* reviewing travel policies *Speaking 2:* introducing changes to work systems *Reading:* cross-cultural contacts

14 Achievements *page 124*

Objective	Topics	Language	Skills work
to describe the achievements of companies and individuals	Corporate development A job advertisement Talking about experience Bad experiences	Present perfect vs. past simple tense *For / Since / Ever / Never*	*Speaking:* executive recruitment *Writing:* an advertisement for your company

15 Systems and Processes *page 134*

Objective	Topics	Language	Skills work
to explain systems and processes in the work place	A leasing system Processes	Passive voice Sequencers	*Listening:* a bakery's ordering process *Speaking:* explaining a flow chart

16 Negotiations *page 142*

Objective	Topics	Language	Skills work
to negotiate a business agreement	Negotiating terms of sale Stating your position Making compromises Hypothesizing	*Would* and *Might* Second conditional *Supposing ...*	*Reading 1:* the stages of a negotiation *Speaking:* negotiating the sale or purchase of a machine *Reading 2:* negotiating skills

1
Meeting People

OBJECTIVE
to meet foreign contacts and get to know them

TASKS

to introduce yourself and other people

to describe jobs and responsibilities

to find out about other people's jobs

to ask questions about foreign companies

to write a personal profile

PRESENTATION

1 Listen to three different conversations. Match each conversation to one of the pictures.

When do we

- shake hands?
- say 'How do you do?'
- say 'How are you?'

2 Are these statements true or false? Listen again and decide.

	T	F

Conversation 1
Mr Velázquez works for Telefónica de España.
Mr Velázquez is responsible for International Accounts.

Conversation 2
Claudette and Sven know each other.
Claudette works for ATT.

Conversation 3
Bob and Luigi work together.
Liz is an engineer.

3 Work in small groups. Practise introducing each other.
Use the phrases below to help you.

Formal	Informal
May I introduce you to . . . ?	*Do you know . . . ?*
Mr Ward, this is Mrs Osborne.	*Michael, this is Sue.*
How do you do?	*Hello.* (British English)
How do you do?	*Hi.* (US English)
Pleased to meet you.	

4 Now practise introducing yourself

- at a reception desk in a company
- to a new colleague
- to an overseas visitor you are meeting at the airport.

These phrases will help you.

Good morning. My name is . . . I have an appointment to see . . . .
I don't think we've met. I'm . . . .
Excuse me. Are you Mrs Wilcockson? I'm . . . .

5 When do we say

- Good morning?
- Good afternoon?
- Good evening?
- Good night?

LANGUAGE WORK

Describing jobs

1 Study the words in blue type in these sentences.

I'm	*a financial controller.* (a/an + job)
	an engineer.

I work for ATT.	(for + employer)

I'm in	*marketing.* (in + type of work)
	the chemicals business.
	chemicals.

2 Complete this dialogue with the correct words.

A So who do you work ....?
B Commodore.
A They're .... computers, aren't they?
B That's right. I'm .... product manager. What about you?
A I work .... Balfour Beatty.
B So you're .... the construction business?
A Yes. I'm .... engineer.

3 Complete these sentences.

1 I'm a/an ....
2 I work for ....
3 I'm in ....

Describing responsibilities

1 Study the organization chart, then complete the description of the organization. If you are not sure of any of the words, check the box at the bottom of the opposite page. Use only one word per space.

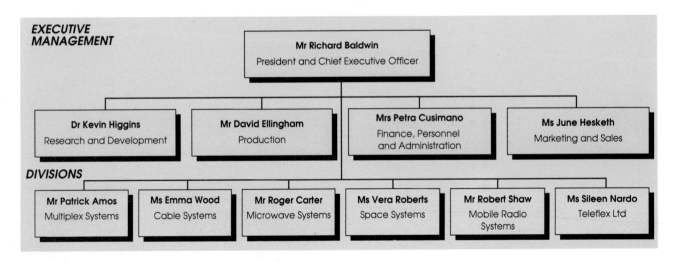

8

> The h......................... of the company is the Chief Executive Officer. He is also the P......................... and a m......................... of the Board of Directors. U......................... him there are four e......................... managers, responsible for research and d......................... , production, f......................... , personnel and administration and m......................... and sales.
>
> The company's activities are d......................... into six business areas, headed by different d......................... managers. These managers r......................... directly to the Chief Executive Officer.

2 Ask and answer more questions about the chart.

Who is	responsible for in charge of	production?	Mr Ellingham.
Who is he responsible to?			The Chief Executive Officer.

3 Find out about your partner.

- Which division do they work in?
- What are they responsible for?
- Who are they responsible to?

Describing tasks

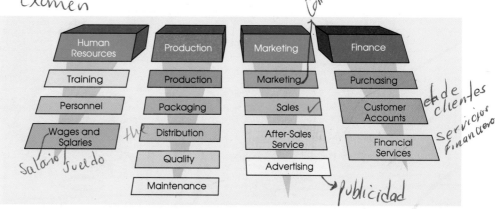

Which department or division

1 buys supplies?
2 sells the products?
3 plans how to sell new products?
4 organizes training courses?
5 recruits new employees?
6 sends the products to the customers?
7 packs the products?
8 manufactures the products?

9 checks the quality?
10 sends invoices to the customers?
11 takes care of the machines?
12 pays the staff?
13 is responsible for after-sales care?
14 deals with taxation, investment, and cash management?
15 runs advertising campaigns?

President	Under	executive	development	marketing	division	head
head	member	Under	executive	finance	divided	report

9

Personal details

acquaintance = Conocido

1 Five visitors are waiting in your company's reception area. Look at their business cards and ask and answer questions about them.

Sustituto
Suplente
comisionado
comisión especial
a una

What's (What is)	his her	name?

What nationality is	he? she?

Who does	he she	work for?
Where does	he she	work?

What's	his her	position in the company?

Swedish

SKANESBANKEN

Birgitte Svensson
Deputy Managing Director

Nybrokajen 7
S - 15146 Stockholm
Tel: 08 663 50 40
Fax: 08 665 40 55

C HEMA Y PUNTO SA

Margarita Vidal Romero
Public Relations Officer
Paseo de la Castellana 201
MADRID
Tel: 1 431 2687
Fax: 1 435 1314
Telex: 45951

Dale Crosby
Vice President
1049 Derwent Drive
Santa Barbara
California
Tel: 805 963 9171
Fax: 805 962 8593

BSCS
Business
Systems
Consultancy
Services

NIHON INFORMALINK KK

Headquarters
Informalink BLDG
257 Akasaka - cho
Tennoji - ku
Osaka 987
Tel: 64 566 3007
Telex: 02423802 INFOKK J

N!

Noburo Yaegashi
Sales Representative

d F
DEUXMONT
FRANCE

Jean Claude Aurelle
Technical Director
238 Rue Socrate
75657 PARIS CEDEX 07
Tel: 78 52 96 34
Telex: 61711 - 49608 D

2 Now find out about the people sitting next to you.

What's your name?
What nationality ......? etc.

3 Put the right question word in the spaces.

WELCOME TO THE CONFERENCE

...*why*... are you here? *To find out about IPQ's newest product.*
...*who*... is it? *The RM110 data communication system.*
...*How*... many people are here? *76.*
...*who*... are they? *European members of the IPQ team.*
...*which*... divisions do they work in? *Marketing and Sales.*
...*when*... do we meet? *At 6 o'clock this evening.*
...*where*... do we meet? *In the Regency Lounge (1st floor).*

Solo

iPQ

| When | Where | Why | What | How | Who | Which |

es mas general
No hay una lista *de opciones*

Cuando hay ungrupode opciones y ya los tenemon

4 Here are some answers, but what are the questions?

1 How do you do?
2 José Pérez.
3 J–O–S–E.
4 I'm Spanish.
5 No, I'm single.
6 IBM.
7 They produce and sell computers.
8 The financial department.
9 I'm an auditor.
10 English, Spanish, and Italian.

What business are they in?
Which department do you work in?

5 Write some questions to ask a colleague.
Ask about

• their company
• their job
• their responsibilities
• their hobbies and interests.

Find someone you don't know very well and ask your questions.

Countries and nationalities

1 *Toshiba is a **Japanese** company. The headquarters are in **Japan**.*
nationality   country

What about these companies?

1 Honda
2 IBM
3 Olivetti
4 Ericsson
5 Norsk Hydro
6 L'Oréal
7 Rolls-Royce
8 Nestlé
9 Siemens
10 Philips

11

Handwritten margin notes (left side):

Preservatives = No tiene conservador
frabic = tela
lecture = Conferencia
attend = Asistir
asist = Atender
Date = Cita o fecha.
trunkl = Destellos
mandatory = obligatorio

What did you major in?
I major in Finance

false cognyt

guardianes

Handwritten answers to exercise 1:
1 Japonesa
2 an American
3 Italian
4 Zurich
5 Norway / Norweigan / Norwegian
6 ~ French
7 Brytes Bredor ENGLAND
8 Zoiz SWISS
9 Germany
10 Holandesa — Holland — Dutch
Switzerland → SWISS
country   Nacionality

Complete the chart.

Country	Nationality
Japan	Japanese
The USA	American
ITALY	Italian
Sweden	Swedish
Norway	Norwegian
France	French
ENGLAND	British
Switzerland	Swiz
Germany	German
The Netherlands	Holland DUTCH

2 Work in pairs. One person uses the table below. The other person uses the table on page 152.

Ask your partner questions to complete the table.

A *Where are the headquarters of Fiat?*
B *In Italy.*
A *So it's an Italian company.*

Hetcuarters
Hetcuarers

RANK BY SALES*	COMPANY	COUNTRY/NATIONALITY
8	Fiat	in Italy / Italian
15	Samsung	South Korea/South Korean
38	INI	Spain / Spanish
39	Petrobras	Brazil/Brazilian
46	Pemex	México / Mexican
63	Petrofina	Belgium/Belgian
88	Alcan Aluminium	Canada / Canadian
104	Broken Hill Proprietary	Australia/Australian
129	Neste	FINLAND/Finnish
143	Koç Holding	Turkey/Turkish

*Position in the *Fortune* list of the 500 biggest industrial corporations outside the US

Turkey = Paco en estadosunidos
gringou = green go (gringo bete)
guiri-guiri (we wee) Intimencian Francesa.

SKILLS WORK

Writing   Read the profile of Derek Stirling and then write another profile about yourself.
Use the topics below to help you.

name   company   responsibilities
nationality   position in the company   free time interests
home town

> **Profile**
>
> My name is Derek Stirling and I'm Scottish. I live in Hadlow, a lovely English village near London, and I work for the Swire group, Britain's largest private company. The Group's activities are divided into five business areas: shipping, aviation, property, industries and trading. Our best-known company is Cathay Pacific Airways.
>
> I work at the London head office, I'm head of Corporate Finance, and I'm responsible for developing the business of the Group.
>
> I'm always very busy and I don't have much free time, but when I do, I like fishing and I grow my own vegetables, just for fun.

Speaking

Ask another person at the conference about their company.	Ask another person where they come from.	You see an old friend. Greet him/her.	Ask another person about their hobbies and interests.
Ask another person at the conference what their job is.			Introduce two people to one another.
Introduce yourself to another person at the conference.			Ask another person about the division or department they work in.
You arrive at the conference hotel. Go to the reception desk and register.	**START**	**INSTRUCTIONS** You are all participants at an international conference. Toss a coin to move – Heads, move one square. Tails, move two squares. Follow the instructions on each square and start conversations. The first person to finish is the winner. **FINISH**	It's time to go home. Give your business card to your new friends and say goodbye.

13

2

Telephoning

OBJECTIVE
to make contact, exchange information, and do business over the phone

TASKS

to give and write down telephone numbers

to spell and note down key words in a telephone message

to make, agree to, and refuse requests

to respond to new situations and say what action you will take

to write business letters confirming telephone calls

to negotiate the sale/purchase of equipment over the phone

PRESENTATION

1 Listen to two different telephone calls and complete the forms below.

Conversation 1

GALAXY COMPUTER SUPPLIES		
SALES PROSPECT		FIRESAFE CABINETS

CUSTOMER DETAILS

NAME	Jose Rosales
POSITION	
COMPANY	EBP
ADDRESS	
FAX	14306687
TEL	

ACTION NECESSARY

send brochure/ sales literature	
send quote	
arrange a sales visit	
phone back	

AREAS OF INTEREST (TICK)

☐ BZ 9   ☐ BZ 10   ☒ BZ 11

Conversation 2

2 Match the words and phrases with similar meanings.

1	The line's busy.	(3)	a	I'll connect you.
2	Will you hold?	(7)	b	One moment.
3	I'll put you through.	(5)	c	An office number
4	A code	(6)	d	Could I have your name?
5	An extension number	(10)	e	I'm ready.
6	Who's calling please?	(1)	f	The line's engaged.
7	Hold on.	(4)	g	A country or area number
8	This is . . .	(10)	h	Is that all?
9	Go ahead.	(2)	i	Can you wait?
10	Anything else?	(8)	j	. . . speaking

3 Listen to the conversations again and answer these questions.

Conversation 1
Why doesn't the switchboard operator connect the caller immediately?
What does the woman say she'll do?

Conversation 2
What question does Marcel Dupont ask about the photoconductor units?
What does Mary Thatcher ask Marcel Dupont to do?

LANGUAGE WORK

Transferring information

1 Study these different ways of saying telephone numbers.

| 34062 | Three four oh six two | (British English) |
| | Three four zero six two | (US English) |

| 95587 | Nine five five eight seven | |
| | Nine double five eight seven | |

Exchange your home and work numbers with your partner. Then dictate these numbers to one another:

29508	071 863 7760
47766	0799 241536
966015	270664
0525 372245	88159
03 916 600721	34067

2 Study the alphabet chart for a few minutes, then try writing it on your own. (All the letters with similar sounds are grouped together.)

1	2	3	4	5	6	7	8
A	B	F	I	O	Q	R	Z
H	C	L	Y		U		
J	D	M			W		
K	E	N					
	G	S					
	P	X					
	T						
	V						

3 Work in pairs. Dictate these abbreviations to one another.

IBM	FOB	OPEC	VIP		WHO	GB	IMF	MBO
EEC	USSR	VDU	GDP		CEO	RPI	EDP	OECD
JAL	AGM	MBA	FBI		VAT	USA	MSc	ICI

4 When you transfer information by phone, try not to leave long silences or pauses. These phrases will help you.

Starting	Ready?	Go ahead.
Continuing	Have you got that?	Got that.
Finishing	Anything else?	That's all.
Checking	Could you read that back to me?	Could I read that back to you?

Work with a colleague. Take it in turns to give each other messages and write them down. One person dictates the messages below and the other dictates the messages on page 152.

Phone Paul Carter tomorrow morning — (03) 408 441932.

Send 200 pieces, ref. no. 306/AJ, to the Siena factory.

Meet Kurt in the Hilton bar at 9.30 pm, Tuesday 14th September.

Requests

1 We use these phrases to ask if it's OK to do things.

Asking	Saying Yes	Saying No
Can I . . . ? *Could I . . . ?* *May I . . . ?*	*Yes, please do.* *Of course.* *Yes, go ahead.* *†Help yourself.*	*I'm afraid . . .* *I'm sorry but . . .*

†Inviting someone to take something

Practise making requests with a partner.

1 You're in a meeting.
    You want to • interrupt when someone's speaking
                • take your jacket off
                • go and make a phone call.

2 You're in a customer's office.
    You want to • use their phone
                • look round their factory
                • smoke.

3 You're in a colleague's office.
    You want to • look at her copy of the production plan
                • borrow her copy of *The Economist*
                • borrow her car.

Spot check

Put *borrow* or *lend* in these questions.

Could you .... me your car?
Could I .... your car?

Notice that we borrow *from* someone and we lend *to* someone.

2 We use these phrases to ask other people to do things.

Asking	Agreeing	Refusing
Can you . . . ? *Could you . . . ?* *Would you . . . ?*	*Yes, certainly.* *Yes, of course.*	*I'm afraid . . .* *I'm sorry but . . .*

You're on the phone. What do you say in these situations?

1 You can't hear the other person.
2 You want them to repeat something.
3 You want them to speak more slowly.
4 You want them to spell a word.
5 You want them to transfer you to the finance department.

Starting the call

Study these phrases for starting calls.

Identifying who is speaking	Saying who you want to speak to
This is Paul Henig.	*Could I* | *speak to . . . ?* *Can I* |
Paul Henig speaking.	*I'd like to speak to . . .*
Is that Julia Gardini?	*Extension 5963, please.*

Supply the missing words in these conversations.

1 **Ms Brunet** Sales Department, good morning.
   Mr Keller .... Helena Steiner, please?
   Ms Brunet Hold on. I'll get her.

2 **Ms Steiner** Hello, Sales.
   Mr Keller .... Helena Steiner, please.
   Ms Steiner ....

3 **Switchboard** Curtis Holdings.
   Mr Keller .... 2938, please.
   Ms Delmont Accounts Department.
   Mr Keller .... Jean Delmont?
   Ms Delmont Yes, ... How can I help
    you, Mr Keller?

Deciding what to do

1 Sometimes we meet new situations or problems and we have to say what action we'll take.

A *The line's busy.*   A *Could you take a message?*
B *I'll call back later.*   B *Hold on. I'll get a pencil.*

Decide what to do in these situations.

A *I'm afraid your train is delayed.*
B *I'll take a taxi.*

1	I'm afraid your train is delayed.	(taxi)
2	The President is busy just now.	(later)
3	We need some more paper.	(order)
4	They don't speak English.	(translator)
5	This quotation is very high.	(another supplier)
6	I have to go to head office tomorrow.	(a lift)
7	They want written confirmation of the order.	(fax)
8	Mrs Bell just fainted.	(water)

2 Sometimes the person we phone is not available.

I'm afraid she's on the other line.
I'm afraid she's in London.
I'm afraid she's on holiday.
I'm afraid he's in a meeting.
I'm afraid he's off sick.

Can you think of more reasons?

Make conversations deciding what to do in these situations.

A *Could I speak to Barbara Morey, please?*
B *I'm afraid she's on holiday this week.*
A *Can you ask her to ring me next week?*

These phrases will help you.

> *I'll hold.*
> *I'll call back later.*
> *Could you | take a message?*
> * | give her a message?*
> *Can you put me through to her secretary?*

SKILLS WORK

Speaking 1   Sit back to back with a partner and act out these telephone calls. One person looks at the information below. The other uses the information on page 152.

Call 1
Your company's new price lists are still at the printers. You expect them to arrive today. A customer calls with a request. Write down the details.

Call 2
Phone your partner and ask them to speak at the GMB congress at Queen Margaret's Hall, Manchester on July 13th. You want them to give a talk on their company's current projects.

Writing   We often write letters to confirm telephone calls. Most business letters contain a lot of standard phrases. Here are some common ones.

The start	The finish	
Dear Sir or Madam	Yours faithfully	(If you don't know the name of the person you're writing to)
Dear Mr / Mrs / Miss / Ms Sloan	Yours sincerely	(If you know the person's name)
Dear Joanna	Best wishes	(If the person is a close business contact or friend)

The reference
With reference to | your advertisement in the *Reporter*, ...
| your letter of 25th April, ...
| your phone call today, ...
Thank you for your letter of March 5th.

The reason for writing
I am writing to | enquire about ...
| apologize for ...
| confirm ...

Requesting Could you possibly ...? I would be grateful if you could ...	**Agreeing to requests** I would be delighted to ...
Giving bad news Unfortunately ... I'm afraid that ...	**Enclosing documents** I am enclosing ... Please find enclosed ...

End the letter with a friendly phrase or a reference to future contact.

Closing remarks

Thank you for your help.

Please contact us again if	we can help in any way.
	there are any problems.
	you have any questions.

Reference to future contact

I look forward to	hearing from you soon.	
	meeting	you next Tuesday.
	seeing	

---

1 Notice how the standard phrases are used in this letter.

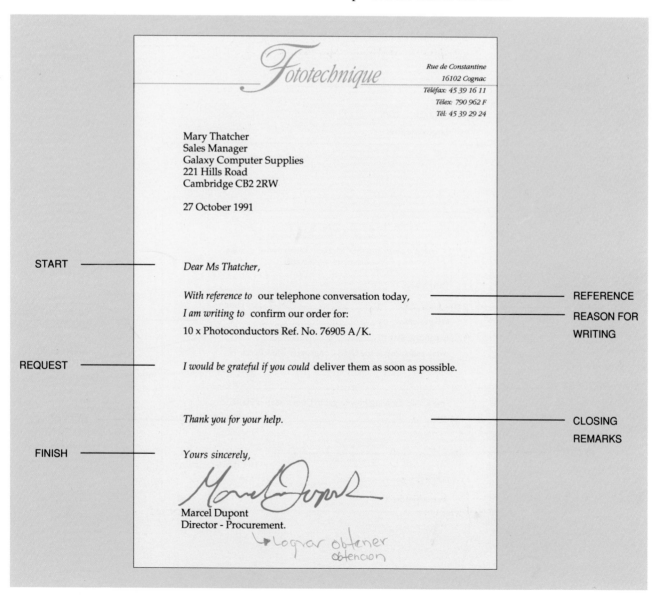

Fototechnique

Rue de Constantine
16102 Cognac
Téléfax: 45 39 16 11
Télex: 790 962 F
Tél: 45 39 29 24

Mary Thatcher
Sales Manager
Galaxy Computer Supplies
221 Hills Road
Cambridge CB2 2RW

27 October 1991

START → *Dear Ms Thatcher,*

With reference to our telephone conversation today, ← REFERENCE

I am writing to confirm our order for: ← REASON FOR WRITING

10 x Photoconductors Ref. No. 76905 A/K.

REQUEST → *I would be grateful if you could* deliver them as soon as possible.

Thank you for your help. ← CLOSING REMARKS

FINISH → *Yours sincerely,*

Marcel Dupont
Director - Procurement.

↳lograr obtener
obtención

2 Use phrases from the list to complete these letters.

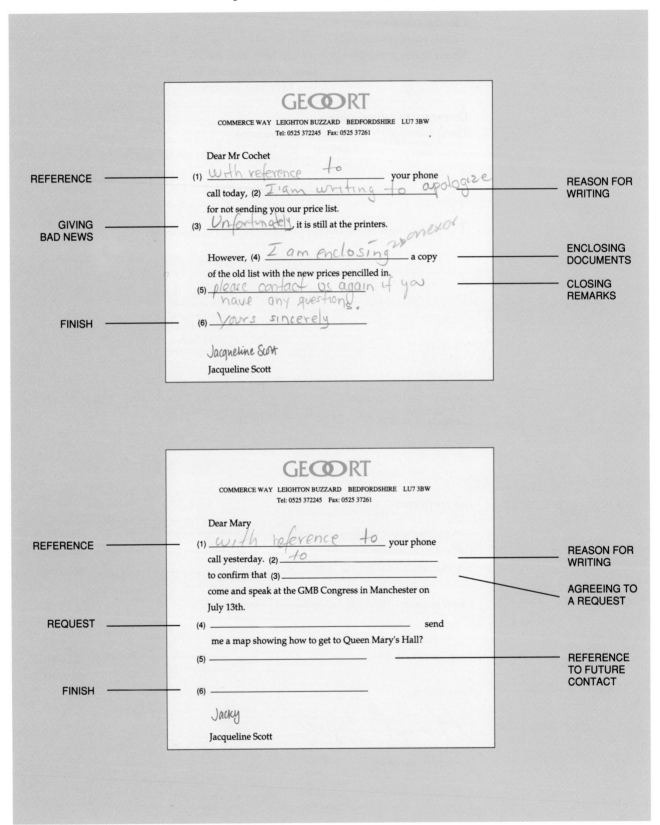

REFERENCE

GEⓍRT

COMMERCE WAY   LEIGHTON BUZZARD   BEDFORDSHIRE   LU7 3BW
Tel: 0525 372245   Fax: 0525 37261

Dear Mr Cochet

REFERENCE
(1) _With reference to_ your phone

REASON FOR WRITING
call today, (2) _I'am writing to apologize_

for not sending you our price list.

GIVING BAD NEWS
(3) _Unfortunately_, it is still at the printers.

However, (4) _I am enclosing_ onexor a copy

ENCLOSING DOCUMENTS

of the old list with the new prices pencilled in.

CLOSING REMARKS
(5) _please contact us again if you have any questions._

FINISH
(6) _Yours sincerely_

Jacqueline Scott

Jacqueline Scott

GEⓍRT

COMMERCE WAY   LEIGHTON BUZZARD   BEDFORDSHIRE   LU7 3BW
Tel: 0525 372245   Fax: 0525 37261

Dear Mary

REFERENCE
(1) _with reference to_ your phone

REASON FOR WRITING
call yesterday. (2) _to_

AGREEING TO A REQUEST
to confirm that (3) _____

come and speak at the GMB Congress in Manchester on

July 13th.

REQUEST
(4) _____ send

me a map showing how to get to Queen Mary's Hall?

REFERENCE TO FUTURE CONTACT
(5) _____

FINISH
(6) _____

Jacky

Jacqueline Scott

Speaking 2   Work in pairs. One person looks at the information below and the other looks at the information on page 152.

You sell computers. A foreign customer phones you. Answer their enquiries about your lap-top computer, the ALT-386SX.
They will ask about

- your prices
- the sales contract
- delivery times
- the guarantee
- discounts
- your terms of payment.

Invent your answers. You can agree to or refuse their requests.
Don't forget to write down their details.

3
Company Presentation

OBJECTIVE

to discuss the business activities of a company

TASKS

to describe current projects

to ask for and give numerical data

to exchange information on facilities

to give a presentation of your company

PRESENTATION

1 Listen to a manager from Philips describing her company and complete these notes.

50 Consumi
50 Profsional and Industial Market

○ 1 Type of products: *Electrical products.* *+ de M*

○ 2 Turnover: *Volumen de ventas en un año.* *24,560M ECUS*

○ 3 Location of the parent *+ de 60* or holding company: *the Netherlands.* *+ Acc. ewla*

○ 4 Number of companies *mundos* in the group: *1,200 Cities ww*

○ 5 Number of employees: *304800*

○ 6 Joint venture partner: *expanding in china whitin people, republic.*
trabajan juntas para produciren producto en especial

24

2 Work in pairs asking and answering questions about Philips. First, write the questions. One word per space.

1 What __does__ Philips produce?
2 What __is__ the group's turnover?
3 __Where__ is the holding company located? _in Netherlands._
4 How many companies __are__ __there__ in the group?
5 __How__ __many__ employees are there?
6 Who __is__ Philips __working__ with in a joint venture?

Tosca

3 Ask each other questions about the companies you work for or about companies you know well.

25

LANGUAGE WORK

Company structure

1 Read the passage below and complete the missing word in each space. If you're not sure of a word, look at the box at the bottom of the page.

> Philips UK Limited m...................... electronic and electrotechnical products for i...................... and private consumers. The company has 16 f...................... in England and Wales and sells its products through r...................... outlets all over the UK.
>
> Philips UK Limited is a s...................... of Philips NV, a m...................... with its h...................... in Eindhoven, the Netherlands. The group employs 304,800 s...................... worldwide and has a t...................... of 24,560 million ECUs.

Current projects

We're working in a joint venture with the People's Republic of China at the moment.

We use the present continuous tense to talk about projects that are going on at the moment.

1 Look at the table below and discuss Philips's current projects with a colleague.

A *What are they doing with Robert Bosch?*
B *They're producing TV studio equipment.*

PARTNER	LOCATION	ACTIVITY
The People's Republic of China	Wuhan	The manufacture of optical glass fibres and cables
	Shenzan	The production of video cassettes
Whirlpool Corporation	USA	The sale of white goods
Matsushita Electronics Corporation	Japan	The manufacture of components
Robert Bosch GmbH	The Federal Republic of Germany	The production of TV studio equipment
Warner Bros. Inc.	USA	The sale of information and entertainment systems

What special projects are going on in your company at the moment?

manufacture	industry	factories	retail	subsidiary	multinational	headquarters
staff	turnover					

26

2 The sentences below all describe actions that are going on at the moment. Complete them with words from the box.
Use the present continuous tense.

| wait | leave | phone | go | build |
| expand | develop | stay | get | spend |

Investigación

1 Philips *are expanding* their activities in China.
2 Our research department *is developing* a new drug.
3 They *are staying* at the Dorchester Hotel.
4 Someone *is waiting* for you in your office.
5 We *are building* a new factory in Barcelona.
6 I *am phoning* about order no. AJ/2496.
7 These products *are getting* near the end of their life cycle. *acercandose.*
8 The dollar *is going* up.
9 The EDP department *is spending* a lot of money on new equipment.
10 I'm tired so I *am leaving* now.

Company profiles

Look at these two ways of using the verb *have*.
A *How many employees has Philips got?*
B *It's got 310,300.*
A *Has it got any factories in the USSR?*
B *No, it hasn't.*

A *How many subsidiaries does Philips have?*
B *It has over 120.*
A *Does it have a subsidiary in the UK?*
B *Yes, it does.*

Practise with a colleague. Ask and answer questions about these companies. (For help with saying numbers, see page 166.)

MATSUSHITA (electronics)	IBM CORPORATION (computers)	SQUARE D (electrical and electronic products)	PAPETERIES DE FRANCE (paper)	CGM (shipping)
170,000 employees	5,000,000 customers	44 factories in the US	10,000 customers	9,000 employees 4,600 at sea 4,400 on land
66 manufacturing companies	383,220 employees	25 manufacturing and assembly plants outside the US	5 warehouses	1,000 agencies and representatives worldwide
34 sales and finance companies	over 100 education centres	18,000 different products in their range	13 sales agencies	77 ships in the fleet

Facilities

DESIGNED FOR THE SMALL TECHNOLOGY-BASED COMPANY

BUSINESS CENTRE

Located in Dundee Technology Park, Prospect House contains 10 office suites on two floors in a beautifully refurbished Victorian house.

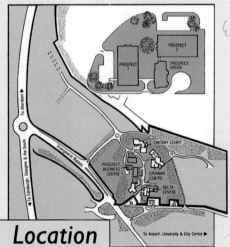

Location

Enterprise Zone. No taxes until 1994.

Flexible lease terms.

Easy access to airport, harbour and railway.

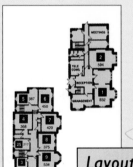

Facilities include:

reception area

conference room

meetings room

fax and telex facilities

mains electricity

gas central heating

Layout Plan

Work with a colleague. Ask and answer questions about Prospect House. Use *Is there . . .?* or *Are there . . .?* Ask about the facilities below.

1 a conference room
2 fax and telex facilities
3 a lift
4 three floors
5 a restaurant

6 gas central heating
7 flexible lease terms
8 tax benefits
9 good transport links
10 air conditioning

Relocation

1 Is your company located in your country's capital city?
What are the advantages of a capital location?
What are the disadvantages?

2 These companies all have head offices outside the capital. Ask and answer questions about them.

What business are Next in?
Where is the company head office?
How far is it from London?
How long does it take to get there | *by train?*
| *by air?*
How many people work at the head office?
Who is the Chairman?
How many days does he spend in London each week?

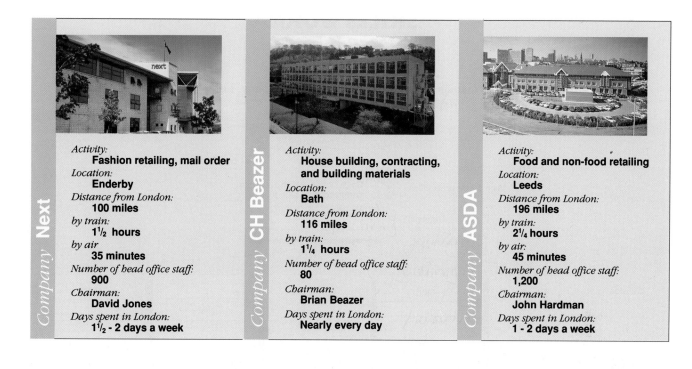

Company **Next**

Activity:
Fashion retailing, mail order
Location:
Enderby
Distance from London:
100 miles
by train:
1¹/₂ hours
by air
35 minutes
Number of head office staff:
900
Chairman:
David Jones
Days spent in London:
1¹/₂ - 2 days a week

Company **CH Beazer**

Activity:
House building, contracting, and building materials
Location:
Bath
Distance from London:
116 miles
by train:
1¹/₄ hours
Number of head office staff:
80
Chairman:
Brian Beazer
Days spent in London:
Nearly every day

Company **ASDA**

Activity:
Food and non-food retailing
Location:
Leeds
Distance from London:
196 miles
by train:
2¹/₄ hours
by air:
45 minutes
Number of head office staff:
1,200
Chairman:
John Hardman
Days spent in London:
1 - 2 days a week

3   Work in pairs. One person uses the information below and the other uses the information on page 153.

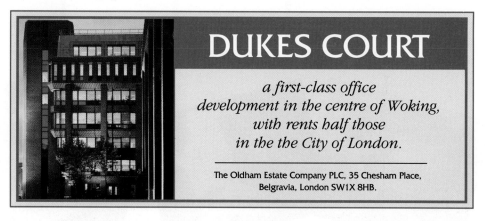

DUKES COURT

a first-class office development in the centre of Woking, with rents half those in the the City of London.

The Oldham Estate Company PLC, 35 Chesham Place, Belgravia, London SW1X 8HB.

Your company is thinking of relocating its headquarters in the country. Ask your partner questions about Dukes Court and complete the notes below.

Dukes Court, Woking	
No. of floors	....
No. of square feet of offices	....
Distance from London – miles	....
– by train	....
Distance from Heathrow Airport – miles	....
– by train	....
No. of lifts	....
Car park	....
Other facilities?	....

SKILLS WORK

Listening   A manager from BICC describes his company. Listen and complete the organization chart below.

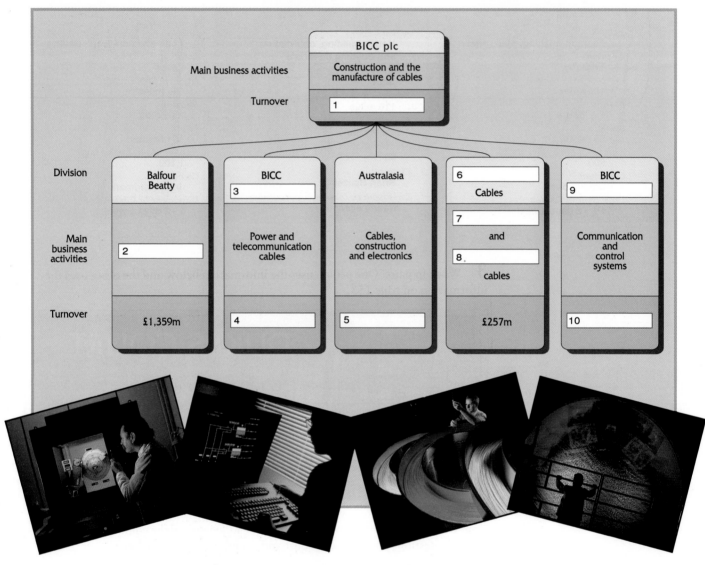

		BICC plc			
Main business activities		Construction and the manufacture of cables			
Turnover		1			

	Balfour Beatty	BICC 3	Australasia	6 Cables	BICC 9
Division					
Main business activities	2	Power and telecommunication cables	Cables, construction and electronics	7 and 8 cables	Communication and control systems
Turnover	£1,359m	4	5	£257m	10

Speaking   **1**   Why is your company special?
What is your company's main strength?

> *We produce high quality products.*
> *We use the most advanced technology.*
> *We are in close contact with the market.*
> *We produce a wide range of products.*
> *We invest a lot of money in research and development.*
> *We have sales representatives all over the world.*
> *Our prices are very competitive.*
> *We are market leaders.*

2 Prepare to give a presentation on your company to the class. Write notes first. Don't write sentences. Just write key words and numbers. (Guess any numbers you don't know.)

	My company	The group
Products/Services		
Main customers		
Locations (factories, branches, etc.)		
No. of employees		
Turnover		
Main strength		
Current projects		
Other information?		

3 Now decide on the structure of your presentation. These phrases will help you order the information.

The introduction	Ordering information
I'd like to tell you about . . .	*I'll begin with . . .* *Now I'll* | *move on* | *to . . .* | *turn* |
Checking understanding	**Finishing**
Is that clear? *Are you with me?* *OK so far?*	*Are there any questions?* *Thank you very much.*

Use your notes to give the presentation and answer questions from your colleagues.

4

Product Description

OBJECTIVE

to describe a product or service

TASKS

to describe things and events using adjectives

to exchange information on size and dimension

to make enquiries about transporting a product

to give an effective description by paraphrasing

to make an informal product presentation

PRESENTATION

1 Saffron Dairies are looking for a new machine to pack milk in cartons. The Technical Manager was in London yesterday to see some 'Tetra Brik' packaging machines in operation. She reports back to the Production Manager.

Look at the sales leaflet and tick (√) the points she covers in her description.

2 Complete the production manager's questions.

1 What .... the trip .... ?
2 Tell me .... the machines. What .... they like?
3 .... breakdowns? .... they reliable?
4 .... the output?
5 How .... are they?

3 Work with a colleague. Imagine you are the Production and Technical Managers. Look at the sales leaflet and act out the conversation again.

TETRA BRIK
aseptic packaging

Machine TBA/8

FEATURES

- *Quiet*
- *Efficient*
- *Safe*
- *Reliable*
- *Easy maintenance*
- *User-friendly controls*
- *Sophisticated technology*

TECHNICAL DATA

- *OUTPUT:*
  6,000 cartons per hour
- *LENGTH: 4.875m*
- *WIDTH: 2.718m*
- *HEIGHT: 5.264m*

LANGUAGE WORK

Description

1

interesting	windy	hot	short
tiring	slow	cheap	old-fashioned
modern	useful	four star	sunny
small	large	expensive	cold
comfortable	efficient	quick	boring
long	dynamic	informative	entertaining

1 *Interesting* is the opposite of *boring*.
Find the opposites of these adjectives in the box:
modern, small, long, slow, hot, cheap.

2 The opposites of these adjectives are not in the box:
comfortable, useful, efficient.
What are they?

2 Which adjectives can describe the items below?

the weather   a hotel   lectures
a journey   people   pubs

(Can you think of more adjectives to describe these things?)

3 Your colleague went on a training course in England. Find out about it. Ask

What | was . . . | like?
     | were . . . |

A *What was the weather like?*
B *It was very cold and windy.*

4 *Interesting* and *interested* are both adjectives.
Interesting describes a quality something has.
Interested describes a reaction.

Complete these sentences.

1 It was an .... meeting.
2 I was very ....
3 There are a lot of .... buildings in Milan.
4 That's an .... idea.
5 We're .... in your products.

5 Do these adjectives describe your products or services?

efficient	reliable	good value
economical	expensive	high-quality

Think of more adjectives to describe your products or services.

Size and dimension

mm

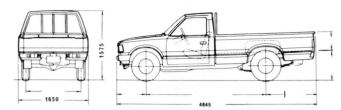

max. load 1,160 kgs
weight 2,570 kgs

1 Study these ways of describing dimension. Then cover them up and try to remember them.

How long is it?	*It's 484·5cm long.*	*The length is 484·5cm.*
How wide is it?	*It's 165·0cm wide.*	*The width is 165·0cm.*
How high is it?	*It's 157·5cm high.*	*The height is 157·5cm.*

How heavy is it?	*It weighs 2,570 kgs.*
How much does it weigh?	

How much can it carry?	*It can carry 1,160 kgs.*
What's the maximum load?	*It's 1,160 kgs.*

2 A transport manager is thinking of buying some Cabstar pick-ups for his fleet. Act out the conversation he/she has with the salesperson. Ask and answer questions about the size and dimension.

mm

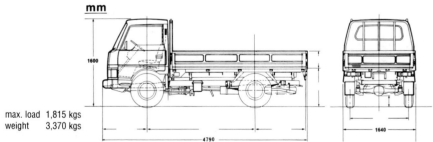

max. load 1,815 kgs
weight 3,370 kgs

3 Work with a colleague. One person looks at the information below. The other looks at the information on page 153.

You want to forward some large steel components to a customer in Rome. Phone your colleague's forwarding company and make enquiries.

> **Your information**
> The components are in 6 wooden crates.
> The dimensions of each crate are:
> Length – 4m   Width – 2m   Height – 2·5m
> The cubic capacity of each crate is 20m³.
> Each crate weighs 1,500 kgs.
>
> **Information required**
> How many trailers do you need?
> How much does it cost?
> How long does it take to drive a trailer to Rome?

Describing what you need

1 Label these photographs using the words in the box.

| microphone | projector | flip chart | lectern | marker | socket |

1 ....

2 ....

3 ....

4 ....

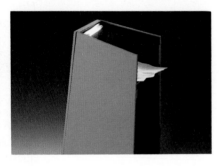

5 ....

6 ....

2 You are preparing to give a presentation at a conference. You need objects to do the things below, but you can't remember their names.

- to show transparencies
- to write on
- to make your voice louder
- to put papers on when you're speaking
- to write with
- to supply electricity

Ask the conference organizer for help.

A *I need a thing to show transparencies.*
B *Do you mean a projector?*
A *Yes, that's right.*

3 Now choose one of the items and describe it to a colleague. They must guess what it is.

A *It's white.*
It's made of paper.
It's similar to a note pad.
You use it to write on.
B *You mean a flip chart.*

SKILLS WORK

Speaking 1

When you don't have the exact word you need in English, you have to find another way of communicating what you mean, using words you do know. So, for example, when you can't remember the word 'newspaper' you have to paraphrase and say 'the thing you read every day in the morning'. It's important to do this quickly to increase your fluency in the language and this exercise practises this skill.

Work with a partner to complete the crossword. One person uses the crossword below and the other uses the crossword on page 153. There are no clues but your partner has the words you need and you have the words he/she needs. You can say anything you like to help your partner, but of course, you can't say the missing word.

Listening   **1**   A sales manager describes a new product to his sales team. Before you listen, label the diagram with the words in the box.

handlebar grips	pull/push handlebars	foot straps
seat	speed and distance meter	

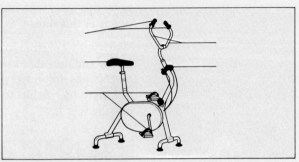

SPECIFICATIONS
Registered design

Length _____

Width _____

Height _____

Weight _____

2   Listen and complete the specifications.

3   Listen again and complete these sentences.

1 The AC4 was very successful ....
2 The AC4 is popular with ....
3 The AC4 doesn't sell well in ....
4 The AC5 is designed for ....
5 The AC5 is suitable for ....
6 The special feature of the AC5 is that it's ....

4   Match the words and phrases with similar meanings.

1 low cost   a strongly made
2 portable   b collapsible
3 high stability   c good value
4 robust construction   d doesn't take up much space
5 compact   e easy to alter or change
6 adjustable   f easy to pick up and carry about
7 folds up for easy storage   g doesn't fall over easily

Speaking 2

Work in groups of four. You all work for the same company. You are looking for executive toys to give your customers and clients this Christmas and you want to give them something unusual.

Each person chooses one product and reads the information about it. Take it in turns to describe your product to the group.

Describe
- its use or purpose
- its size and dimensions
- the accessories (extras) it comes with
- the price.

Decide what to buy your customers.

Omnibot

The electronic butler

Just the thing to impress your clients and friends.

In the morning he comes quietly into your room and wakes you up with your favourite music. He brings you your morning tea with the daily paper and responds to your commands by remote control. At the office he shows visitors around and at parties he delivers hors d'oeuvres to your surprised friends.

Strong plastic body and quiet rubber wheels. Comes with:
- a built-in rechargeable battery
- a programme module
- full instructions

Approx. 30cm x 30cm x 50cm
£199.00

Off the wall

Tennis ball alarm clock

Just the thing to help you get up on Monday morning.

It's 7 o'clock in the morning and your alarm clock starts to ring. But you've got 'Off the wall'. You reach over, pick it up and throw it against the wall. It falls silent. You get up feeling better. What a wonderful way to start the day!

'Off the wall' is a 10cm diameter shock proof electronic alarm clock. It comes complete with its own stand.

(Batteries not supplied)
£9.95

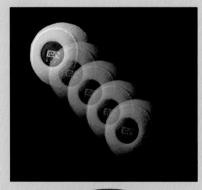

ProGolf

Just the thing to keep a golf fan happy on rainy days.

ProGolf is an advanced microchip electronic golf game for one or two players. Each player has a set of 12 golf clubs to choose from as they go round the course, complete with bunkers and lakes. Perfect speed and timing are necessary to win and the game is a sensation with serious (and not so serious) golfers.

Comes with full instructions and batteries.

A colour booklet provides a map of each hole.

18cm x 8cm x 2cm   Weight 180 g
£49.95

Language translator

Just the thing to take with you on your next foreign business trip.

Here is the world's first multilingual pocket translator. It contains over 8,000 words in 5 different languages. Just type in a word, press the button and it gives you an instant translation. Perfect for business travellers. Small enough to put in your pocket or

handbag, and so light it can travel with you wherever you go.

The memory contains more than 1,600 words in each language.

14cm x 6cm   Weight 100 g
(Batteries not supplied)
£34.95

5
Reporting

OBJECTIVE

to report on past actions

TASKS

to talk about events in a company's history

to explain when things happened

to establish what happened on a business trip

to read about product launches and discuss what went wrong

to give an account of a project in your workplace

PRESENTATION

1 You will hear a manager describing the history of a product development project. Listen to the tape and number these actions in the order they happened.

☐ modify the designs
☐ run a feasibility study
☐ send the drawings to potential customers
☐ run tests
☐ shelve the project
☐ design and construct the prototype
☐ prepare detailed drawings

2   Listen to the tape again and make a note of when these things happened.

| 1 FEASIBILITY STUDY | | 2 PROTOTYPE DESIGN |

3 TESTS

| 5 DESIGN MODIFICATION | 4 PREPARATION OF DETAILED DRAWINGS AND SPECIFICATIONS |

3   What problems did they have

1   at the test stage?
2   at the drawings and specifications stage?
3   at the design modification stage?
4   at the manufacturing stage?

41

LANGUAGE WORK

Company history

THE HISTORY OF THE NISSAN MOTOR COMPANY

1925

Three small motor companies merge to form the Dat Jidosha Seizo Company.

1947

After World War II, Nissan begins car production again.

1932

The company produces the first Datsun car.

1958

A Datsun 210 wins the Australian Rally.

1934

The owners rename the company 'The Nissan Motor Company Ltd'.

NISSAN MOTOR CO., LTD.

1966

Nissan sets up its first foreign manufacturing operation in Mexico.

1935

Nissan opens the Yokohama plant.

1980

Nissan buys a stake in Motor Iberica SA of Spain.

1936

Nissan introduces mass production methods.

1981

Nissan makes an agreement with Volkswagen to produce the Santana in Japan.

1938

Nissan stops producing passenger cars and concentrates on truck* manufacture.

1986

Nissan builds its first factory in the UK.

*British English – Lorry

---

1   Work in pairs. Ask and answer questions about the history of the Nissan Motor Company.

A   *What happened in 1925?*
B   *Three small motor companies merged.*
A   *What happened in 1947?*
B   *Nissan began car production again.*

Notice that regular verbs end *-ed* in the past tense. Irregular verbs have a special form. There is a table of irregular verbs on page 168.

2   Complete these questions.

A   When .... the original three companies .... ?
B   In 1925.
A   When .... Nissan .... the first Datsun car?
B   In 1932.
A   When .... the owners .... the company?
B   In 1934.

We usually use *did* to make a question in the past tense. The main verb doesn't change to a past form.
      Work in pairs. Ask and answer more questions about the history of the Nissan Motor Company.

3   Choose the correct verbs from the boxes to complete the passage. Remember to put them into the past tense.

have	grow
import	sell
be(×2)	

decide	become
begin	find

achieve	start
export	rise
supply	have to
can	

The History of Nissan UK Ltd.

Nissan UK Limited was founded in 1969. At first, it .... just a trading company. It .... cars from Japan and .... them in the UK. In 1970, the company .... only 0.2% of the UK car market but the company .... fast. By 1974 they .... the UK's leading car importer.

When the UK .... one of Nissan's main export markets, the company .... to build an assembly plant here. After a long search, they .... a suitable site in Tyne and Wear. Cars .... rolling off the production line in 1986.

At first, the plant .... limit production because of the JAMA import restriction agreement. But by 1988 UK companies .... the majority of components and Nissan .... the target of 60% local content. The plant .... increase production.

The plant .... assembling cars for the continent as well as the UK. In 1988, they .... 11,000 Nissan Bluebirds to Europe. In 1990, the figure .... to over 100,000.

---

4 Work in pairs. One person uses the information below and the other uses the information on page 153.

You are a newspaper reporter writing an article on Facit – a Swedish office equipment company. Ask the Public Relations Officer for information to complete your notes.

When did Facit begin manufacturing furniture?
What happened in 1928?

1413	started trading as a copper mining company
....	began manufacturing furniture
1928	....
....	acquired Halda typewriters
....	first introduced their products into the USA
1950	....
1956	....
....	launched the "Facit System 80" range of office furniture
1973	....
....	sold the Facit Data Systems business to Data Saab
....	launched their first laser printer
1986	....
....	became a subsidiary of Entranor

Saying when things happened

1 Notice the prepositions we use with these times:

In 1984   *At* the end of '88   *On* Friday 15th.

Which preposition do we use for the times below?

		example				example
1	Years	*1999*	6	Seasons		*winter*
2	Days of the week	*Saturday*	7	Parts of the day		*the afternoon*
3	Dates	*Easter*	8	Religious festivals		*Easter*
4	Months	*August*	9	Points in time		*the end of the war*
5	Hours of the clock	*5.30 p.m.*				

2 Put the right preposition with these times.

1	 1969	7	.... Christmas
2	.... Thursday	8	.... Christmas Day
3	.... 19 January	9	.... the autumn (*US*: the fall)
4	.... January	10	.... the 1960s
5	.... midnight	11	.... the weekend
6	.... the morning	12	.... the turn of the century

Finding out what happened

1 Find out about your partner's last business trip. (Your partner can tell the truth or invent answers.) First write some questions.

Town/country	Where .... ?
Method of transport	.... travel?
Journey time	How long .... ?
Accommodation	Where .... ?
Length of stay	.... stay?
Purpose of trip	Why .... ?
Opinion of trip	Was .... successful?

2 Your American associate company launched a new product last year. You want to write an article about it for your company magazine. First, write some questions to get the information you need.

Type of product	What .... ?
Time it took to develop	How long .... ?
Size of investment ($)	How much .... ?
Launch date	When .... ?
Advertising media	Where .... ?
Advertising budget ($)	What .... ?
Sales in the first six months	How many .... ?

Work in pairs. Take it in turns to ask and answer the questions. The answers are in the box below, but be careful. They are not in the right order.

$7.2m	Television & magazines	8,000,000
A slimming machine	May 12th	12 months
$12.5m		

45

SKILLS WORK

Reading

1   Sometimes products don't sell well in a new market. Suggest what went wrong in these cases.

---

1   Western companies had problems selling refrigerators in Japan until they changed the design to make them quieter.

2   In Saudi Arabia, newspaper adverts for an airline showed an attractive hostess serving champagne to happy passengers. A lot of passengers cancelled their flight reservations.

3   A soap powder advertisement had a picture of dirty clothes on the left, a box of soap in the middle and clean clothes on the right. The soap didn't sell well in the Middle East.

4   A company had problems when it tried to introduce instant coffee to the French market.

5   Several European and American firms couldn't sell their products in Dubai when they ran their advertising campaign in Arabic.

6   An airline company called itself Emu, after the Australian bird. But Australians didn't want to use the airline.

7   A TV commercial for a cleaning product showed a little girl cleaning up the mess her brother made. The commercial caused problems in Canada.

8   A toothpaste manufacturer couldn't sell its product in parts of South East Asia.

9   An American golf ball manufacturer launched its products in Japan packed in boxes of four. It had to change the pack size.

10   A ladies' electric shaver sold well throughout Europe, but not in Italy.

---

2   Here are the reasons for the problems, but they are in the wrong order. Number them from 1 to 10.

☐   In Japanese the word for 'four' sounds like the word for 'death'. Things don't sell well packed in fours.

☐   People thought the commercial was too sexist and reinforced old male/female stereotypes.

☐   Unveiled women don't mix with men in Saudi Arabia and alcohol is illegal.

☐   90% of the population came from Pakistan, India, Iran and elsewhere, so Arabic was the wrong language.

☐   It seems Italian men prefer ladies' legs unshaven.

☐   The advertisers forgot that in that part of the world, people usually read from right to left.

☐   The people in this area didn't want white teeth. They thought darkly-stained teeth were beautiful and they tried to blacken them.

☐ Japanese homes were small and sometimes walls were made of paper. It was important for the refrigerators to be quiet.

☐ Making 'real' coffee was an important part of the French way of life. Instant coffee was too casual.

☐ The emu can't fly.

How many reasons did you get right?

3 Scanning

Look through the passages again and find the words below.

1 An abbreviation for the word *advertisement*
2 The word for an advertisement on television
3 A word that means *marked* or *discoloured*
4 The name of a bird
5 The name of a sport
6 The name of a language

Speaking

Think of a project you took part in at work, for example

- the launch of a new product/service
- a product development project
- the design/introduction of a new system
- a construction project
- setting up a new venture/operation
- a training programme.

1 What were the objectives or goals of the project?
2 List the tasks you performed to achieve those objectives.
3 How long did each task take?
  How long did it take to complete the project?
4 What were your main problems?
  How did you solve them?
5 What were the results of the project?

Work in small groups. Take it in turns to explain your projects to the group and answer questions.

6
Socializing

OBJECTIVE
to hold social conversations with business contacts

TASKS

to welcome an overseas visitor

to order food at a business lunch

to make, accept, and refuse offers

to discuss leisure interests

to read and discuss an article on executive life styles

PRESENTATION

1 **In the office**

1 Kevin Donoghue is welcoming a client, Paolo Farneti, to his office. Listen to the dialogue. Are these statements true or false?

	T	F

a This is their first meeting.
b Kevin gave Paolo directions.
c The journey took two hours.
d Paolo wants white coffee.

2 Act out their conversation with a partner. The pictures below will help you remember it.

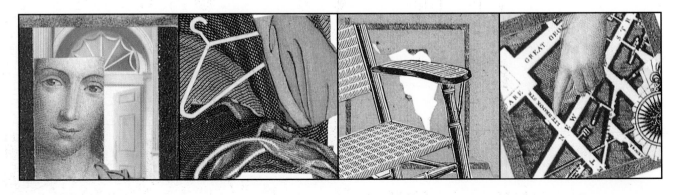

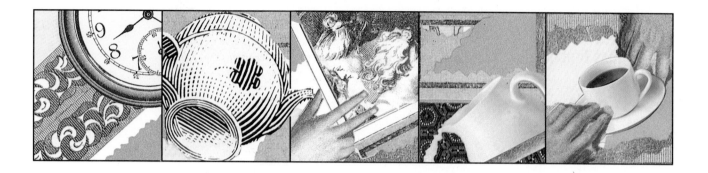

2 In the car

1 Kevin is driving Paolo to a restaurant. Listen to the dialogue. Are these statements true or false?

	T	F
a This is Paolo's first visit to Cambridge.		
b Kevin offers to show Paolo round next week.		
c Kevin plays golf.		
d Paolo goes skiing once a month in winter.		

a This is Paolo's first visit to Cambridge.
b Kevin offers to show Paolo round next week.
c Kevin plays golf.
d Paolo goes skiing once a month in winter.

2 Imagine you're welcoming a visitor to your home town. Act out a similar conversation. Complete this dialogue first.

A Is this your first visit to .... ?
B Yes, ... I'd love to see ....
A .... show you round tomorrow after the meeting?
B That's very kind .... Is there a good .... here?
A Yes, there is. .... interested in sport?
B Yes. I play .... and I go .... What about you?
A I ....

3 In the restaurant

Kevin and Paolo are ordering wine in a restaurant. Before you listen, read the dialogue below and guess the missing words. Use one word per space.

Waiter   The wine list sir.
Kevin   Thank you. Let's see. What .... of wine do you like, Paolo?
Paolo   I .... white.
Kevin   .... or dry?
Paolo   Dry.
Kevin   Then let's have the Chablis. It's usually very good.
Paolo   How .... do you come here?
Kevin   About once a month.
           (*to the waiter*)
           Excuse me.
Waiter   Yes sir?
Kevin   We'll .... the Chablis please. Number 63.
Paolo   And I'd .... a bottle of mineral water too please.

Listen to the conversation and check your answers.

LANGUAGE WORK

Business lunches **1** Match the dishes on the menu to the pictures.

Menu

STARTERS
Smoked Salmon
*Slices of best Scottish salmon served with
brown bread and butter*
Cheese Tart
Light crisp pastry with a creamy cheese filling
Garden Soup
A delicate summer vegetable soup with herbs

MAIN COURSE
Duck with Green Peas
Duck stewed with spices, herbs and freshly picked peas
Dover Sole
*Poached and served in a cream sauce with prawns
and asparagus tips*
Roast Leg of Welsh Lamb
*Flavoured with garlic and rosemary, and served
with onion sauce*

PUDDINGS
Summer Pudding
*A classic combination of summer fruits
(cherries, raspberries, black- and redcurrants) and bread*
Strawberries and Cream
Our own fresh English strawberries
Chocolate Fudge Cake
A rich, sticky chocolate cake

CHEESE
A wide selection of English cheeses
Liqueurs
Coffee

2 Put these different foods into the right category.

| peas | lamb | pork | sole | salmon | duck |
| raspberries | chicken | cauliflower | strawberries | beef | cherries |

Meat	Fish	Poultry	Vegetables	Fruit

Think of more words to add to each category. What is your favourite meal?

3 Work in small groups. Appoint someone as the waiter/waitress and give them your orders.

I'll have the cheese tart.
Salmon for me. What about you John?
I'd like the duck.
Garden soup please, and I'd like Dover Sole to follow.
What do you suggest?

Offering things **1** You can make uncountable nouns countable by using *a* .... *of* ....

wine ———— *a glass of wine*

bread ———— *a piece of bread*

Find the uncountable nouns in the pictures below. Make them countable.
Use phrases like *some cake* or *a piece of cake*.

2 Look at the words in blue print in these sentences.

Would you like a biscuit? (**a** + singular countable noun)

Would you like some wine? (**some** + uncountable noun)

Would you like some grapes? (**some** + plural countable noun)

For more information on countable and uncountable nouns, see page 165.

Take it in turns to offer food and drink.

Offering		Saying yes	Saying no
Would you like	*a . . . ?* *some . . . ?*	*Thanks.* *Yes please.* *I'd love* | *one.* | *some.*	*No thanks.* *It looks lovely but . . .*

Offering help

You are entertaining a visitor from abroad. He/She is called back home unexpectedly, and must leave as soon as possible.

Work with a colleague. Take it in turns to play the visitor and the host. Use pronouns, for example *it, them, him, her*.

A *I need to change my flight.*
B *Shall I change it for you?*
A *No, it's all right thanks. I'll manage./*
Oh, yes please. That's very kind of you.

1 change my flight
2 tell Maria to postpone tomorrow's meeting
3 cancel my hotel booking
4 fax the division reports to Lisbon
5 ask Stephan to pick me up at the airport
6 phone Mr Parry and cancel Friday's appointment
7 give the trading figures back to the Financial Director
8 thank Claire for all her help this week

Interests and routines

1 Work in pairs. Find out about your partner's interests.

What	*sort* *kind* *type*	*of*	*books* *films* *music*	*do you like?*

I like . . . No me guston
I don't like . . . No me guston
I love . . . las amo me encanton
I hate . . . odio no me gustan

detective stories novels biographies history books others?	musicals thrillers comedies westerns others?	jazz pop music classical music folk music others?

GO *GO* *GO* *GO*

play *play*

COURT
cancha

2 1 Put the sports above with the right verb in the table below.

Play *jugar*	Go *ir*	Do *hacer*
SOCCER	SWIMMING	YOGA
TENIS	WINDSURFING	KARATE or YUDO
GOLF	RUNNING AND	WEIGHTLIFTING
	YOGGING	

2 Think of some more sports. Which verbs do they go with?
3 What sports do your colleagues take part in? Ask them.

Do you	play squash?	Yes, I do	Where do you	play?
	go cycling?	No, I don't. Do you?		go?
	do yoga?			do it?

3 Find out about a colleague's routine.

How often do they

1 entertain customers or clients?
2 use English at work?
3 work overtime?
4 attend meetings?
5 travel abroad on business?
6 go jogging?

How often do you . . . ?

Every	day	Once	a	week
	two weeks	Twice		year
	month	Three times		

4

I always read the *Financial Times*

I usually read the *Economist*

I often read *Time* magazine too

I sometimes read the *Wall Street Journal*

I don't often watch television

I never watch cartoon films

Find out about the person sitting next to you.

- What newspapers do they read?
- What magazines and journals do they read?
- What TV programmes do they watch?

Social chit-chat

1 Social quiz

Decide which replies are possible. (More than one may be OK.)

1 'Hello. How are you?
   a I'm very fine, thank you.
   b Not too bad.
   c Fine thanks, and you? ✓

2 'This is Stewart Edwards.'
   a How do you do?
   b How are you?
   c Pleased to meet you. ✓

3 'Did you have a good trip?'
   a Yes, thanks. ✓
   b Yes, of course.
   c Well, I had a few problems. ✓

4 'Would you like to see round the factory?'
   a Yes, I will.
   b Yes, I'd love to. ✓
   c No.

5 'Do you want to buy some?'
   a Well, I'm interesting.
   b Well, I'm interested.
   c Yes, I want. ✓

6 'Why are you learning English'?
   a For talking to my customers.
   b For to talk to my customers.
   c To talk to my customers. ✓

7 'Would you prefer red or white wine?'
   a I prefer red. ✓
   b I don't care.
   c I don't mind. ✓

8 'Is Thursday convenient?'
   a What means *convenient*?
   b What does *convenient* mean? ✓
   c Could you explain me *convenient*? ✓

9 'I'm terribly sorry about that.'
   a You're welcome.
   b Don't mention it.
   c Don't worry about it. ✓

10 'Thank you very much.' ✓
   a Not at all.
   b It doesn't matter.
   c It was a pleasure. ✓

2 When you meet people for the first time, it's nice to find you've got things in common. Work with a colleague. Do you both play golf? Do you both have the same number of children? Find five things you've got in common.

54

3   You go to a reception at an international conference in London. Talk to the other participants. Think of different replies.

4   Match these replies to the right comment.

a   Yes please. I'll have a gin and tonic.
b   Yes, it is. I didn't expect all this traffic.
c   It's very good of you but I'd like to walk.
d   Cheers!
e   That's right. I'm from Brazil.
f   Cheerio then. See you tomorrow.
g   It's Emma. Emma Tanner.

h   Yes it is, isn't it?
i   Don't worry. I'll have an orange juice instead.
j   The Sheraton. It's not far from here.
k   Very good indeed, thank you.
l   Thanks. They look delicious.

SKILLS WORK

Speaking

You are having lunch with a foreign visitor to your company. You need to keep the conversation going.
What subjects are easy to talk about?
What subjects are interesting to talk about?
What other subjects do you enjoy talking about? Add them to the list.

	Easy	Interesting
The work/business you are doing together		
Your jobs		
Your families		
Your home towns		
Sports		
Your hobbies and interests		
The weather		
Items in the news		
Films		
Your holidays		
Politics		
Religion		
Love		

Find a colleague and compare your lists. Find a subject you both find interesting and have a conversation.

Reading

1 Before you read, imagine a typical British business executive.

What sports does he like?
What's his favourite drink?
What sort of home has he got?
What sort of car does he drive?
What does he do in the evenings?

Now read the article on the next page and see if you are right.

2 Comprehension check

1 What does a typical British executive do after dinner?
2 What kinds of people did the researchers interview?
3 What sorts of cars do European executives buy?

56

HIGHFLYING TASTES

The average British Executive has a game of squash or swim after work. Then he goes home to his detached house, washes up after dinner and sits down in front of the television with a scotch.

This is according to a survey on the different lifestyles of business people in 13 different countries. Researchers for the Pan European survey interviewed 8,604 professional people with a high income, education level or occupational status. Those interviewed were all aged between 25 and 74 and most of them were in the 35 – 44 age group.

The survey found that European executives have very different attitudes to life, but there is one thing on which they all agree. They are all patriotic when buying a car.

The British prefer Austin Rover and Ford, the French have Citroens and Peugeots, the Germans have BMWs and Mercedes and the Italians have their Alfa Romeos and Fiats.

HOW THE EXECUTIVE LIFESTYLES COMPARE

	Great Britain %	France %	West Germany %	Italy %	Nether-lands %	Spain %	Sweden %	Switz-erland %
Television								
Watch under 7 hours	24.6	42.0	46.4	45.9	58.9	45.4	38.1	65.2
7 - 14 hours	46.9	30.4	39.1	36.7	32.6	35.3	43.3	15.1
15 hours or more	25.9	11.0	11.6	11.8	4.5	13.4	12.8	0.9
Watch foreign stations	1.8	5.9	25.5	14.7	76.6	6.0	11.9	75.1
Watch cable/satellite	2.2	3.3	18.7	1.7	44.0	4.5	10.9	22.8
Luxuries								
Own video recorder	65.5	40.0	44.2	29.9	40.7	48.2	42.0	34.5
Video camera	7.2	8.7	9.7	9.7	4.6	19.4	10.7	11.6
Comapct disc player	16.7	25.4	28.2	26.2	23.7	44.2	17.2	34.6
Car telephone	6.2	2.8	3.6	1.4	3.7	1.6	16.1	2.5
Yacht/cruiser/speedboat	4.6	3.1	3.9	8.6	9.0	8.0	26.1	5.2
Swimming pool	0.9	3.8	7.5	1.6	0.2	28.6	3.4	5.6
Sauna	0.5	0.9	17.5	0.5	0.5	2.6	34.4	6.0
Wear designer clothes	18.2	38.5	32.4	28.8	24.1	15.1	27.2	31.2
Leisure								
Foreign holidays	50.6	34.2	70.1	33.8	63.8	31.6	42.0	56.8
Visits to cinema	26.7	49.1	25.8	39.3	28.7	67.3	29.8	35.5
Art galleries, museums	28.6	37.4	35.3	39.4	32.1	36.2	32.6	41.6
Going to the theatre	35.4	24.5	40.3	30.5	33.3	32.0	32.1	33.8
Swimming	65.5	42.8	56.2	44.1	42.6	49.9	36.6	50.7
Cycling	24.1	29.4	52.2	12.9	33.6	11.6	13.3	30.8
Tennis	23.1	31.9	33.8	28.4	33.4	33.4	21.1	26.1
Drinking/Smoking								
Scotch	93.6	57.5	30.4	64.	56.6	43.9	85.0	54.3
Cognac	39.7	29.9	47.3	25.5	43.9	17.5	46.8	50.7
Champagne	32.1	62.8	32.7	23.3	20.3	16.7	27.2	42.8
Port	45.0	41.1	27.5	29.8	34.9	15.9	49.1	24.6
Non-smokers	72.2	49.0	58.6	49.3	53.3	42.9	60.1	54.3

3 Talking about statistics

Ask a colleague questions about the statistics.

A *How many German executives go abroad on holiday?*
B *Seventy point one per cent.*

4 Is your country on the chart?

Yes? Do you think the statistics are accurate?
No? What do you think the statistics are in your country?

5 Conducting a survey

Write the questions the interviewers asked the executives.

How many hours do you spend watching television each week?
Do you watch any foreign stations?

Then use your questions to interview a colleague.

7
Meetings

OBJECTIVE
to discuss corporate problems and decide what action to take

TASKS

to state alternatives and recommend action

to ask for the opinions of your colleagues

to discuss future plans and justify decisions

to make, reject, and accept suggestions

to hold a meeting to discuss a new venture

PRESENTATION

Three managers discuss the recruitment of sales representatives (reps) for their new Spanish sales organization.

1 Listen and note their reaction to the alternatives. Write *F* if they are for them and *A* if they are against them.

Alternatives	Marcel	Carlos	Nancy
recruit new Spanish Sales reps			
transfer French Sales reps			

58

2   Listen again and complete these minutes of the meeting.

```
              THE NEW SPANISH SALES ORGANIZATION              Page 3

Alternative 1
Take on new Spanish sales representatives and (1) _____ .
Alternative 2
Teach our French sales reps Spanish and (2) _____ .

The advantage of Alternative 2 is the French sales staff have already
got (3) _____ . The disadvantage is it takes (4) _____ .

The disadvantage of Alternative 1 is that it takes a year to (5) _____
On the other hand it is a Spanish (6) _____ so we should employ
Spanish (7) _____ .
```

3   Match these phrases from the dialogue to the correct box below.

a I don't agree.	**g** What do you think?
b Why don't we . . . ?	**h** The important thing here is . . .
c Any views on this?	**i** How do you feel about that proposal . . . ?
d I think we should . . .	**j** We can either . . . or . . .
e I don't think we should . . .	**k** It's a waste of time.
f We need to discuss . . .	

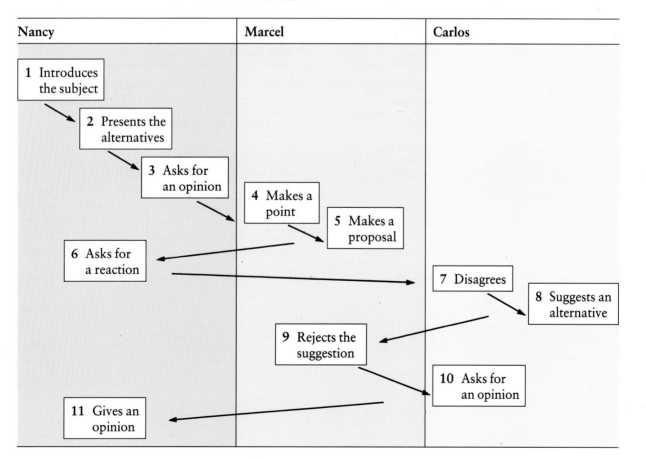

Nancy	Marcel	Carlos
1 Introduces the subject		
2 Presents the alternatives		
3 Asks for an opinion		
	4 Makes a point	
	5 Makes a proposal	
6 Asks for a reaction		
		7 Disagrees
		8 Suggests an alternative
	9 Rejects the suggestion	
		10 Asks for an opinion
11 Gives an opinion		

Now listen to the dialogue again and check your answers.

LANGUAGE WORK

Recommending action

1 Notice the word *should* in this sentence.
I think we should teach the French sales staff Spanish.

The speaker is recommending action.

Recommend action in these situations.

Begin: *'I think we should . . .'* and *'I don't think we should . . .'*

1 You have a machine that is old and often breaks down.
2 Your market share is falling.
3 One of your suppliers often sends you invoices with several mistakes on them.
4 The company's main warehouse is too small.
5 Your main competitors are cutting their prices by 20%.
6 An employee is often absent from work. He says he's ill but you don't believe him.

2 Work in pairs. You are colleagues meeting to discuss some of your company's problems. Take it in turns to start discussions on these subjects.

A *We need to discuss . . .*
   Basically we've got two alternatives:
   we can either . . . or . . .
B *I think we should . . .*

Problem	Alternatives	
company English classes	employ a teacher	send the staff to a language school
the paperwork	buy another computer	recruit a secretary
company cars	rent them	buy them
the pay deal	offer a 10% salary increase	offer 5% and a productivity bonus
office cleaning	employ cleaners	contract the work out
the new sales job	promote someone	contact a recruitment agency

3 Your company must reduce its running costs by £1,000,000. Look at the proposals below and decide what to do.

```
ESTIMATED SAVING

1    Cut the research and development
         budget:        by 5%         £400,000
                        by 10%        £800,000


2    Cut the staff training
         budget:        by 10%        £200,000
                        by 20%        £400,000


3    Cut the advertising
         budget:        by 10%        £350,000
                        by 20%        £700,000


4    Stop all donations to charity:    £100,000


5    Make the company security staff redundant
     and subcontract the work:        £150,000


6    Close the company health centre: £100,000


7    Cancel the plans to buy:
         new production machinery     £200,000
         new EDP equipment            £150,000
```

4 Discuss your choices with some colleagues. Ask for their opinions.

Do you think	*we should . . . ?*	*Yes, I do.*
		No, I don't.
I think . . .		*I agree.*
I don't think . . .		*I don't agree.*

How do you feel about this?
What do you think about this?
Have you got any views on this?

61

Justifying decisions

Your company wants to improve the quality of its product/service. Your boss wants you to organize regular meetings to discuss ways to achieve this objective. Decide how the meetings should be run.

[handwritten annotations: quiere, incrementar, tarea, descargar, jefe, como deben ser las juntas]

1 Are you going to
   a invite staff from all levels of the organization?
   b just invite managers?
   c *I going to just invite managers*

2 Are you going to
   a decide who should attend?
   b ask for volunteers?
   c *I going to ask for volunteers*

3 Are you going to
   a hold the meetings once a week?
   b hold the meetings once a month?
   c *I going to hold the meetings once a week*

4 Are you going to
   a hold the meetings in office hours?
   b hold the meetings in the evenings or at weekends?
   c *I going to hold the meetings in office hours*

5 Are you going to
   a keep the meetings short?
   b allow the meetings to go on as long as necessary?
   c *I going to allow the meetings to go on as long as necessary*

6 Are you going to
   a allow people to smoke?
   b stop people smoking?
   c *I going to stop people smoking*

Justify your decisions to a colleague.

A *Why are you going to . . . ?*
B *I'm going to . . . because . . .*
   I'm not going to . . . because . . .

Grammar note

Notice we use *going to* to talk about our intentions, or things we plan to do in the future. For more information on future forms, see page 162.

Making suggestions

1 Study these ways of making suggestions.

Making suggestions	Accepting	Rejecting
Why don't we . . . ? *Shall we . . . ?* *We could . . .*	*That's a good idea.* *Yes, let's do that.* *Great.*	*Yes, but . . .* *That's a good idea but . . .* *I'm not sure about that.*

Practise the phrases with a colleague. Suggest solutions to the problems below.

Follow this pattern:

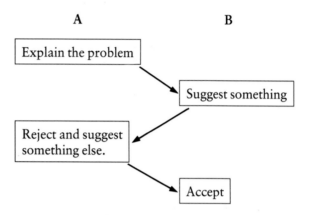

1 You need to improve your staff's level of English. What can you do?
2 Your company's results show an unexpected $500,000 profit on international currency deals. Suggest things to do with the money.
3 You need to think of a name for your new brand of toothpaste. Suggest some alternatives.
4 You want to recruit some new, young staff – school-leavers perhaps. How can you find them?
5 Your company was founded 100 years ago. You want to mark the occasion. Suggest ways to celebrate.

2 Work in groups of three or four. Each group works for a different bank. Your bank wants to attract young customers – aged between 5 and 18. It's your job to think of promotions that will attract these young people. The bank is prepared to spend a lot of money if they think your ideas will work.

You have 10 minutes to think of something before you report back to the class and tell everyone what you're going to do.

SKILLS WORK

Listening

1 The directors of a hotel group discuss the financial problems of one of their hotels. Record the views of three different people at the meeting. Write a number (1 for Kim, 2 for Oscar, 3 for Miranda) opposite each opinion.

1 Kim/Oscar/Miranda rejects the idea that the main problem is

    □   a   investment.
    □   b   price.
    c   c   bad management.

2 He/She thinks the main problem is

    □   a   marketing.
    □   b   investment.
    □   c   location.

3 He/She thinks they should

    □   a   cut back services.
    □   b   develop the conference trade.
    □   c   upgrade the hotel.

4 This means they

    □   a   can increase prices.
    □   b   have to improve the hotel's facilities.
    □   c   can reduce prices.

2

1 The chairperson didn't know what Kim meant by *upgrade*. What did he ask?
2 He didn't know what Oscar meant by *wrong location*. What did he ask?
3 Miranda thought the question of price was not important. Complete her comment:
    I think --

3 Match these words and phrases from the discussion to the correct explanation.

1 upgrade   a   reductions, savings
2 returns   b   good situation or location
3 cut-backs   c   time of year when the hotel doesn't have many guests
4 budget   d   make better, improve
5 off season   e   rooms, equipment, etc. for a particular activity or purpose
6 prime site   f   money received back from an investment
7 booming   g   low price
8 facilities   h   growing, increasing

Speaking Your company is building a new hotel in a city centre of your choice. It will have

- 376 double bedrooms
- 106 single bedrooms
- 7 suites.

Hold a meeting to decide what facilities and services the hotel should offer. You can elect a chairman if you wish.

First, study the phrases below. They will help you control the discussion.

Starting
Shall we get started?
We need to discuss . . .

Moving on
Shall we move on to . . .?
Let's turn to . . .

Asking for clarification
What do you mean by . . .?
I didn't follow what you said about . . .

Coming back to the main point
I think we're getting side-tracked.
Can we get back to the main point?

Checking agreement
Are we all agreed?
So we're going to . . .

Now look at the points below and decide what to do.

1 What sort of guests do you want to attract to the hotel?

- Business travellers
- Conference guests
- Tourists – coach parties
            – family groups
            – couples
            – single people

2 What image should the hotel have?

- Businesslike and efficient
- Friendly and welcoming
- Grand and luxurious
- Good value for money
- Anything else?

3   What style of decor should the hotel have?

Modern and high-tech

Old-fashioned

Glamorous

Exotic

4   What facilities should the hotel have? You have enough space and money to choose one item from each box below.

Japanese-style garden
Minigolf course
Three outdoor tennis courts
Outdoor swimming-pool

Hairdresser's
Gift shop
Library/Writing-room

Indoor swimming-pool
Shopping arcade
Discothèque

Gymnasium with weight-training equipment
Two squash courts
Sauna
Indoor tennis court

5 What bars and restaurants should the hotel have? You have enough space for three of the following:

- French restaurant
- Local cuisine restaurant
- Chinese restaurant
- Seafood restaurant
- Cocktail bar
- Snack-bar
- Tea/Coffee lounge
- Pub
- Another type of bar/restaurant

6 What services should the hotel offer?

- 24-hour reception desk
- Nightly shoe cleaning
- Laundry and dry cleaning
- Hourly bus service to the airport
- 24-hour room service
- 24-hour restaurant service
- Daily bus trips to places of interest
- Secretarial services
- Anything else?

7 Think of a special promotion event for the hotel's opening.

8

Making Arrangements

OBJECTIVE
to make and change arrangements

TASKS

to explain future plans and arrangements

to fix a time and place for a meeting

to invite business contacts to social events

to read and write telex messages arranging a visit

to arrange a schedule for a visit

PRESENTATION

1 Listen to three telephone calls Alan Wilson received and fill in the details in his diary opposite.

2 Listen to the three calls again and answer these questions.

Call 1
1 Patrick invites Alan to play golf. What does he say?

....

2 At the end of the call he confirms the arrangement. What does he say?

....

Call 2
1 Mrs Lonsdale invites Alan to her office to see some plans. What does she say?

....

2 Why can't Alan go on Friday?
3 At the end of the call she confirms the arrangement. What does she say?

....

Call 3
1 Cristina tells Alan she can't keep her appointment on the 16th. What does she say?

....

2 Why can't Alan meet her on the 18th? What does he say?

....

68

3 After the last phone call, Alan picked up the phone and made another call. Who did he ring and what did he say?

LANGUAGE WORK

Timetables, plans, and arrangements

1 *My flight leaves at 2.15.*

We often use the present simple tense to talk about timetables.

Work with a partner asking and answering questions.

A   *When does the London train leave?*
B   *It leaves at 11.20.*

The London train	leave	11.20 a.m.
	arrive	3.45 p.m.
The board meeting	start	3.00 p.m.
	finish	5.15 p.m.
The bank	open	9.30 a.m.
	close	3.30 p.m.

2   Now look at the conference programme and ask about:

- the Regional Performance Reports
- shuttle buses to the airport
- *Mange Tout* Restaurant
- the roof-top barbecue
- *Highlights* hairdressers
- coach tours of the city

IAMT CONFERENCE
Programme for July 22nd

9.30am   Regional Performance
Reports: Germany
Italy
Scandinavia
Marlborough Room
Conference Suite 6th Floor

12.30pm   Lunch
Swithins Restaurant
3rd Floor

2.30 pm   Regional Performance
Reports: The USA
Hungary
Spain
Marlborough Room
Conference Suite 6th Floor

8.00pm - Midnight   Roof Top Barbecue with the 'Hill Runners Jazz Quartet'
Riverside Hotel
Roof Garden

SHUTTLEBUSES TO THE AIRPORT

Riverside Hotel offers a regular daily service to Heathrow and Gatwick. Coaches leave from the main entrance at **7.00, 10.00, 13.00, 16.00 and 19.00**

Please allow 60 minutes for your journey to Heathrow and 90 minutes for Gatwick

MANGE TOUT RESTAURANT

French Cuisine
Lunch 12 noon - 2.30pm
Dinner 7.00pm - 11.00 pm
The restaurant is located in the Florence Arcade on the Ground Floor. Patrons are kindly requested to reserve a table in advance to avoid disappointment.
(0751) 248260

Highlights
Unisex Hairdressers
9.45 am–5.30 pm
Florence Arcade
Riverside Hotel
0751-248197
No appointment necessary

COACH TOURS OF THE CITY

Twice daily tours
10.30 - 12.30
2.30 - 4.30

£8 adult £5 child
Please book at reception

3   *I'm flying to Chicago on Friday.*

We use the present continuous tense to talk about future plans and arrangements.

Look at the itinerary below. Ask and answer questions about Mr Gruber's schedule.

A   *When is he arriving?*
B   *At nine o'clock.*
A   *What's he doing first?*
B   *He's meeting the Overseas Sales Manager in the conference room.*

ITINERARY FOR THE VISIT OF MR. H. GRUBER TO THE
LEYTONSTONE FACTORY
25 JULY

9.00	Arrival
9.05-9.45	Meeting with the Overseas Sales Manager (Conference Room)
9.45-10.15	Company presentation video
10.15-10.45	Coffee with the Marketing Director and Finance Director
10.45-11.45	Demonstration of the N4 prototype
11.45-12.40	Meeting with the Managing Director and Marketing Director (Boardroom)
12.40-2.30	Lunch with the Overseas Sales Manager (Saraceno Restaurant)
2.30-3.30	Tour of Leytonstone factory
3.30-4.00	Final discussions with the Overseas Sales Manager
4.00	Car to Terminal 2, Heathrow Airport
6.00	Flight to Frankfurt, LH 1607

Making appointments

1   Put these sentences in the correct order to make a short conversation.

☐   Yes, please. Would Tuesday the 26th be convenient?

☐   It's quite all right. I'll look forward to seeing you on Thursday the 28th, then.

☐   I'm calling about our appointment on the 25th. I'm afraid I can't make it.

☐   Thank you. Goodbye.

☐   Yes, I can manage the 28th. I'm sorry to be a nuisance.

☐   It doesn't matter. Would you like to fix another time?

☐   I'm afraid I'm tied up on the 26th. How about the 28th?

71

2 Supply alternative words for these phrases. Use words from the conversation.

1 We need to | arrange
| f............................ | a time for the next meeting.

2 Are you free | next Wednesday?
H............................ |

3 I'm afraid I'm | busy.
| t............................ up.

4 When would | suit you?
| be c............................?

5 I can | make
| m............................ | Friday.

6 I'm afraid I can't | come
| m............................ it | to Tuesday's meeting.

Invitations 1

Inviting	Saying Yes	Saying No
Would you like to . . .?	*Thank you. I'd like that.* *That would be lovely.*	*I'd love to, but . . .* *I'm sorry, but . . .*

You are entertaining a foreign visitor from your parent company. Ask if they want to

- come to the monthly marketing meeting
- give a talk at the meeting
- meet the production manager
- see the new packaging machinery
- come to a party.

Fixing a time

1

Suggesting a time

Can you	make manage	2 o'clock on Thursday?
Are you free	on at	the 26th? 3.30?
How about		

Saying Yes
Yes, that suits me. *Yes, I'm free.* *Yes, that's fine.*

Saying No

I'm afraid	I can't	make manage	it.
		I'm tied up.	

Practise the phrases in pairs. Use the pattern below.

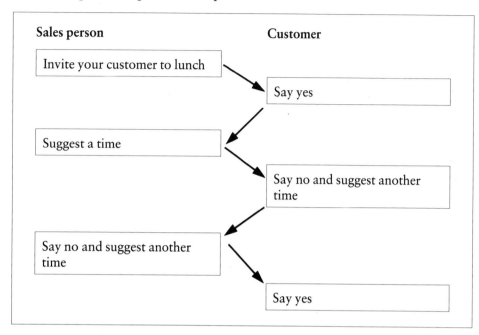

Now practise again. The sales person should invite the customer to
- visit a local tourist spot
- come to dinner
- come to a nightclub.

2 You want to arrange a meeting with the people sitting next to you. Arrange a time and place that suit everyone.

Asking for suggestions			Confirming
When What time Where	*would*	*suit you?*	*I'll look forward to seeing you on Thursday at ten, then.*
		be convenient for you?	*See you on Thursday at ten, then.*

3 Work in pairs. One person should look at the information below and the other should look at the information on page 154.

You want to arrange a meeting with your colleague. Phone him/her and arrange a time and place. Here is your diary for next week.

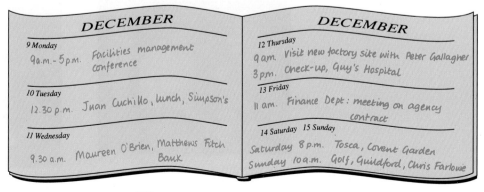

Invitations 2

Inviting	Saying Yes	Saying No
Do you feel like . . . (-ing)?	*That's a good idea.*	*Well actually . . .*
How about . . . (-ing)?	*Yeah, great.*	*I'm afraid . . .*

Compare these phrases with the ones on page 72. Which are more informal?

```
                  tomorrow              at the weekend
NOW ──────────────────────────────────────────────── THE FUTURE
          tonight    the day after tomorrow    next week
```

Ask a colleague about their future plans. If they're free, invite them to do something with you.

A *Are you doing anything special tonight?*
B *No, not really. I'm just going home and watching TV.*
A *How about coming out for a drink?*
B *That's a good idea.*

Here are some ideas of things to do.

SKILLS WORK

Reading and Writing

1 Telex messages and email (messages between computers) contain a lot of abbreviations. What words are abbreviated in this message?

```
05 10 91 12.34
+104846 +
RE 104846 G
KTC 0747 KT

TO DARWORTH ENTERPRISES

ATTN JANET JEFFRIES
RE INSPECTION VISIT
ARR FLGT NO JL401
TERML 3 HEATHROW JUN 16 ETA 1635.  CLD U BK HOTEL
ACC FOR 3 NIGHTS IN CTY CENTRE.  ALSO PLS ARR MTG
WITH DATA LINK FOR JUN 17 IF POSS.
MANY TNKS
NAKAGAWA
```

To save time, typists often miss small words from telexes. What words are missing in the message above?

2 Telex and email messages are very short. Abbreviations save time, but sometimes they are difficult to understand. You have to look at the whole sentence to understand the meaning.

What do the abbreviations mean in the messages below?

1 FAO MRS SUSANNA BURN
2 FWDING SAMPLES TODAY. EXPECT DEL NEXT TUES.
3 REF YR LTR DATED JAN 9
4 RE OURTELCON YESTERDAY, PLS FWD CONTRACT DOCS SOONEST.
5 15% IS MAX DISCOUNT. OK?
6 WE CFM FERNANDEZ ARR 17 JAN NOT 16. WLD U CHNG HOTEL RESERVATION.
7 RGT WE NEED MORE INFO BFOR WE CAN QUOTE.
8 WILL TLX TOMORROW N ADV ETA.

You can check your answers in the telex abbreviations on page 169.

3   These words are often missing in telexes and email:

- articles (*the, a, an*)
- prepositions (*in, at, on,* etc.)
- pronouns (*we, your, me, it, his, this,* etc.)
- parts of the verb *be* (*are, is, was, were,* etc.)

Rewrite these messages missing out words. Use abbreviations if you can, but make sure the message is still clear.

1   THE DOCUMENTS ARRIVED YESTERDAY.
2   WE EXPECT A DELIVERY NEXT WEEK.
3   COULD YOU SEND AN ITINERARY?
4   THE TRAIN ARRIVES IN TURIN AT 14.20.
5   SEE YOU ON FRIDAY.
6   WE RECEIVED YOUR ORDER NO 8914. THANK YOU.
7   ROMANEZ ARRANGED A MEETING WITH ME BUT HE HAD TO CANCEL IT BECAUSE HIS CAR BROKE DOWN.
8   WE ARE ARRIVING ON TUESDAY AT 10 A.M. IS THIS OK? PLEASE ADVISE US AS SOON AS POSSIBLE IF THIS IS NOT CONVENIENT.
9   WE ARE SORRY WE DIDN'T TELEX YOU YESTERDAY. THERE WAS A PUBLIC HOLIDAY AND THE OFFICE WAS CLOSED.
10   THE SHIPMENT WAS LATE AND TWO PARTS WERE MISSING.

4   Work in two groups. One group is writing telexes for Janet Jeffries. They should use the information below.
The other group is writing telexes for Mr Nakagawa. They should use the information on page 154.

Group 1
Write a reply to Mr Nakagawa's telex from Janet Jeffries. (One person in the group should write and the others should dictate and check spellings.)

Your message
You will meet Mr Nakagawa at Heathrow at 16.35 on June 16. You booked a single room in the Hyde Park Hotel for Mr Nakagawa for 2 nights.
Is this OK?
You want Mr Nakagawa to advise you if his wife is coming too.
You will change the booking if she is.
You arranged his meeting with Data Link for June 17th.
Tell him you'll see him next week.
Send your regards and sign the telex 'Janet Jeffries'.

You will also receive a telex from the other group. Write a reply.

Speaking   Work with a partner. One person should use the information below and the other should use the information on page 154.

1   You are visiting your UK subsidiary for three days next week. You have two lunch-time appointments but you also want to arrange meetings with the people on this list.

Names	Time needed for meeting
Mrs Carne	3 hours (must see her on Monday morning)
Mr Gandhi	2 hours
Miss Carley	3 hours
Mr Barnes	4 hours (Factory tour)
Ms Lyon	2 hours (wednesday if possible)

Phone your colleague in the UK and arrange your schedule. Pencil in the times.

21 Monday	9-10 am	
	10-11 am	
	11-12 am	
	12-1 pm	} Lunch with Dave Csernovicz
	1-2 pm	(Barclays Bank)
	2-3 pm	
	3-4 pm	
	4-5 pm	
22 Tuesday	9-10 am	
	10-11 am	
	11-12 am	
	12-1 pm	} Reception, Barbican Centre
	1-2 pm	
	2-3 pm	
	3-4 pm	
	4-5 pm	
23 Wednesday	9-10 am	
	10-11 am	
	11-12 am	
	12-1 pm	
	1-2 pm	
	2-3 pm	
	3-4 pm	
	4-5 pm	

2   Your boss has just told you about an important meeting at head office next Wednesday so you must catch the 6 a.m. flight home on Wednesday morning.

Phone your colleague in the UK again. Explain your problem and rearrange your schedule.

You can cancel your visit to the reception but you can't cancel your appointment with Dave Csernovicz.

Describing Trends

OBJECTIVE

to describe and discuss figures and graphs

TASKS

---

to describe changes in a company's finances

---

to give reasons for changes in performance

---

to write divisional performance reports

---

to describe and explain trends in your workplace

PRESENTATION

1 Complete these graphs.

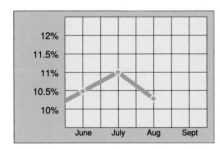

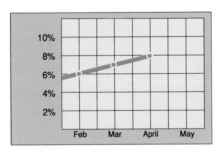

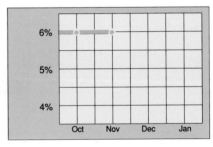

1 The rate of unemployment increased to 11% in September.

2 Interest rates decreased by 2% in May.

3 Inflation went down from 5.5% in December to 5% in January.

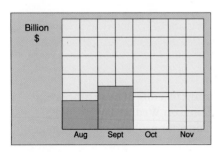

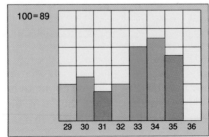

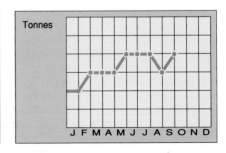

4 Consumer spending rose sharply in November.

5 The retail price index went up slightly in week 36.

6 Production fell steadily in the last quarter of the year.

2 Listen to a sales manager describing his company's sales figures and complete the graph below.

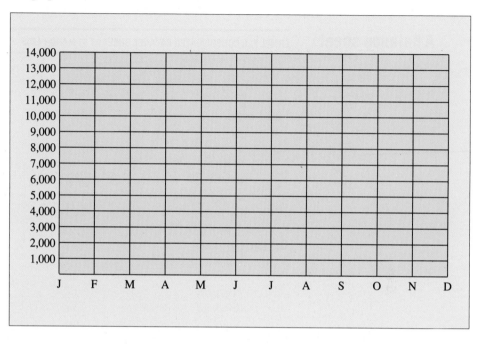

3 Listen again and note why these things happened.

1 Sales increased in March.

----

2 Sales fell in May.

----

3 Sales rose in July.

----

4 Sales increased in September.

----

5 Sales went down in November.

LANGUAGE WORK

A balance sheet

ERMEL PLC CONSOLIDATED BALANCE SHEET AT 31 MARCH 1992

	_1991_	_1992_
	£m	£m
Fixed assets	133	130
Current assets		
stocks	61	72
debtors	82	98
cash in bank	26	—
	169	170
Current liabilities		
loans and overdraft	1	21
creditors	46	48
taxation	17	21
dividend	34	6
	98	96
Net current assets	71	74
Total assets	204	204
Share capital and reserves	204	204

1 Match these explanations to items on the balance sheet.

1 Amount Ermel owe the bank
2 Investment in the business by shareholders
3 Property and equipment
4 Amount Ermel will give to the shareholders
5 Amount they owe their suppliers
6 Amount their customers owe them
7 Raw materials, work in progress, and finished goods
8 Current assets minus (−) current liabilities
9 Fixed assets plus (+) net current assets

2 Complete these sentences about Ermel's balance sheet. Use a preposition (_to, from, by, at,_ etc.)

1 The amount they owed their creditors increased .... £46 .... £48m.
2 The dividend decreased .... £28m.
3 Share capital and reserves remained steady .... £204m.
4 Taxation increased .... £21m.
5 The amount their debtors owed them rose .... £82m .... £98m.
6 Total assets stayed .... £204m.
7 Their loans and overdraft increased .... £20m.

3 Use prepositions to complete the sentences below:

1	We	invested	a lot of money	.... the business.
2		spent		.... training courses.
3		wasted		.... unnecessary equipment.
4		earned		.... our overseas investments.
5		saved		.... our energy bills.
6		gave		.... charity.
7		borrowed		.... the bank.
8		owed		.... our suppliers.

Describing changes

1 Discuss last year's figures with a colleague. One person should use the information on the left and the other should use the information on the right.

Use these verbs.

increase   rise   go up   decrease   fall   go down

A   *Our market share fell by 1 per cent last year.*
B   *Yes, but on the other hand our turnover increased by 8 per cent.*

Our market share	−1%		Our turnover	+8%
Sales to the EEC	−2%		Exports to Japan	+5%
The number of new products	−6%		Spending on research and development	+9%
Distribution costs	+18%		Prices of raw materials	−4%
Spending on training	+26%		Customer satisfaction	+27%
The number of employees	−4%		Productivity	+6%
Wages	+15%		The number of days lost through industrial action	−80%
Energy bills	+5%		Energy costs per unit	−1%
Share prices	−9%		Dividends	+10%

2 Write six sentences about your company's figures for last year, similar to the examples below.

Our turnover increased by 50 million francs.
The number of employees went up by 5 per cent.

1 ....
2 ....
3 ....
4 ....
5 ....
6 ....

3 Complete these tables.

Verb (action)	Noun (thing)
to rise	a rise
to fall	
to increase	
to decrease	
to improve	
to recover	

Adjective (describes a noun)	Adverb (describes a verb)	Type of change
slight	slightly	very small
sharp		sudden, large
dramatic		sudden, very large
steady		regular (not sudden)

4 Study the graph and use each adjective once to complete the description.

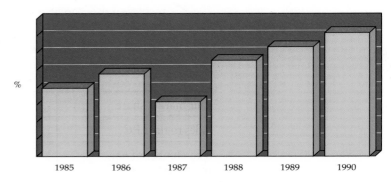

We had a (1) .... increase in market share in 1986, followed by a (2) .... fall in 1987 when we sold a brand. But a successful new brand launched in 1988 meant there was a (3) .... recovery that year and a (4) .... increase in 1989 and 1990 too.

5 Now use each adverb once to complete this description.

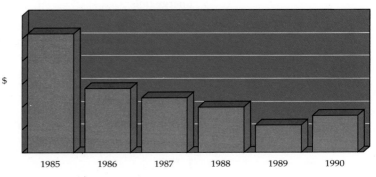

Our production costs per unit fell (1) .... in 1986 when we automated the assembly line and they continued to decrease (2) .... for the next three years.
They went down (3) .... in 1989 when we bought the new packaging machinery but rose (4) .... in 1990 because of increased time spent on quality control.

6 Now use each adjective and adverb once to complete this description.

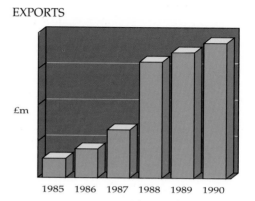

UK SALES

EXPORTS

Sales to the UK market rose (1) .... between 1985 and 1987.
There was a (2) .... decrease in 1988 when our main distributor
went out of business. Sales recovered (3) .... in 1989 and the
(4) .... improvement in 1990 brought us back to the 1985 level.
There was a (5) .... rise in exports in 1986. They went up
(6) .... in 1987 when we began to break into the US market.
They rose (7) .... in 1988 when we signed the new agency
agreements and there was a (8) .... increase in 1989 and 1990.

Describing graphs

Work in pairs. One person should use the information below and the other
should use the information on page 155.

The graph below shows a company's sales over a 12-month period. Describe it to
your colleague.

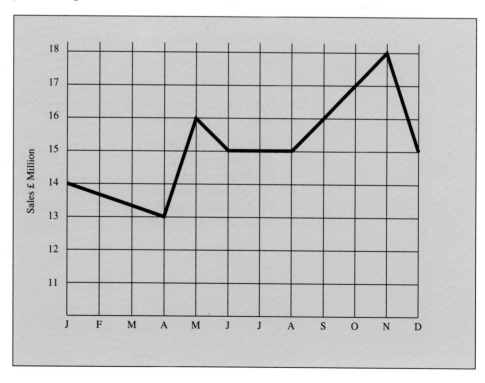

Now listen to your partner's description of the energy costs of a smaller company over a period of 12 months. Complete the graph below.

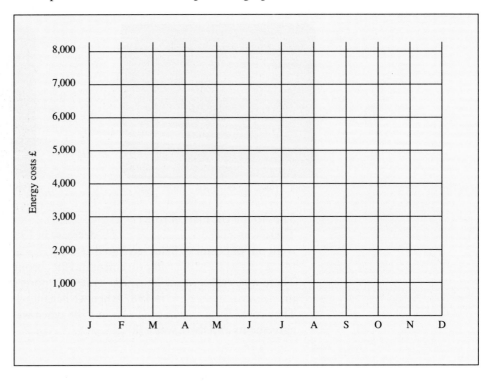

Giving reasons

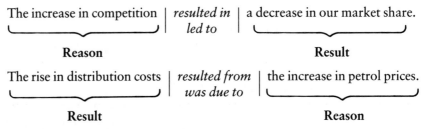

The increase in competition | *resulted in* | a decrease in our market share.
led to

Reason — Result

The rise in distribution costs | *resulted from* | the increase in petrol prices.
was due to

Result — Reason

Study the phrases below. Which are reasons and which are results? Link them with one of the phrases above.

1 The factory automation .... an increase in productivity.
2 The staff reductions .... the factory automation.
3 The large pay rises   .... a decrease in staff turnover.
4 The increase in sales costs .... the rise in spending on advertising.
5 The big orders from Japan .... a recovery in sales.
6 The shorter delivery times .... the new distribution system.

SKILLS WORK

Writing

1988 was year of success and achievement for the BP Group. We focused on core businesses and developed our sound strategic base.

A fall in oil prices led to a decrease in profits, but there was an increase in oil and gas production.

The acquisition of Britoil resulted in increased access to oil reserves.

We can look forward to the years ahead, confident of further growth.

Peter Walters
16 February 1989.

Study the operating profit figures and background information. Write a short report on the performance of each division. Use the examples below to help you.

BP Chemicals
A sharp increase in demand for petrochemicals led to a dramatic rise in operating profit.
or
The dramatic increase in operating profit was due to a sharp rise in demand for petrochemicals.

DIVISION	OPERATING PROFIT (LOSS)		BACKGROUND INFORMATION
	1988 £m	1987 £m	
BP Exploration	1,381	1,977	There was a fall in the average price of crude oil from $18.5 a barrel in 1987 to $15 in 1988.
BP Oil	769	474	There was a recovery in the oil refining business.
BP Chemicals	514	227	There was a sharp increase in demand for petrochemicals.
BP Minerals	304	126	There was heavy capital expenditure and investment.
BP Nutrition	14	52	There was a fall in market prices for chicken, eggs, and pigs.
BP Coal	20	(29)	There was a growth in coal-fired electricity generation and record levels of steel production.

Listening

1 You are going to listen to a report on the performance of the UK economy in the 1980s.

Before you listen, match the explanations below to one of the economic indicators on the chart.

1 The cost of borrowing money
2 The cost of borrowing money for home purchase
3 Goods bought from abroad
4 Goods sold abroad
5 The general increase in prices
6 The number of people without work
7 The money people spend
8 The money a government spends

A *balance of trade* shows the difference between a country's imports and exports. A positive sum (+) in the balance of trade is a *surplus*. What is a negative (−) sum?

Economic Indicator	Explanation No.	Movement
Inflation		
Unemployment		
Consumer spending		
Public spending		
Imports		
Exports		
Interest rates		
The mortgage rate		

2 Now listen to the report. Note the movement of the economic indicators in the chart above. Was it up (↑), down (↓), or both (↑↓ or ↓↑)?

Listen again and complete these notes with figures from the report.

1 The rate of inflation was .... in 1986.
2 Unemployment reached .... in the mid eighties.
3 Consumer spending increased by nearly ....
4 There was a surplus of nearly £............................... in the balance of trade in 1986.
5 There was a deficit of over £............................... in the balance of trade in 1987.
6 The mortgage rate rose from .... in 1988 to .... in 1990.

3 What happened in your country's economy

● in the 1980s?
● last year?
● last month?

Speaking Draw a graph representing something connected with your work, for example

- seasonal sales trends
- annual turnover
- raw materials prices
- number of employees.

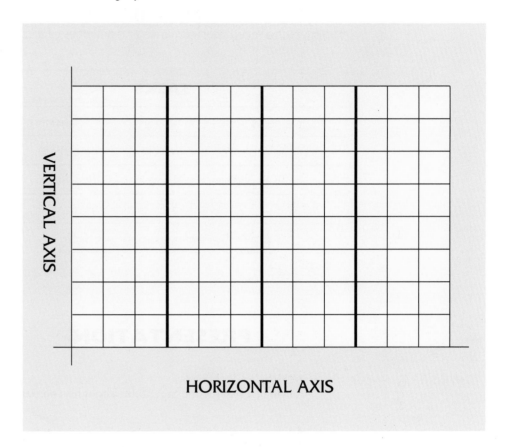

Take it in turns to present your graphs to the group. Explain what they represent. Give reasons for the changes.

The phrases below will help you. So will the phrases on page 31.

This graph shows . . .
As you can see . . .
This led to . . .
This was due to . . .
Are there any questions?

10
Company Results

PRESENTATION

A manager from Kobe Steel talks about his company's performance this year.

1 Listen and complete the notes below.

> **Global Activities**
> Created a new .... (Kobe Steel USA Inc.)
> Entered into a .... with the USX Corporation
> Opened new research centres in ....
>
> **Results**
> Sales this year: ¥ ....
> Net income this year: ¥ ....
>
> **The New Kobe '88 Plan**
> Target reduction in the labour force: ....
> Actual reduction in the labour force: ....
> Target reduction in inventory: ....
> Actual reduction in inventory: ....

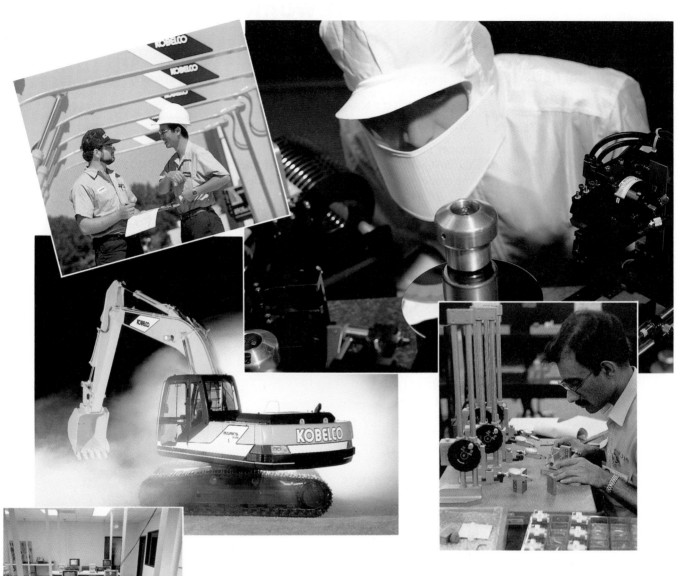

2 Complete these sentences with verbs from the box, then listen again and check your answers.

1 Kobe Steel .... its global activities this year.
2 We .... a new wholly-owned subsidiary.
3 Our financial results .... excellent.
4 Net income .... to ¥21.6 billion.
5 We .... our targets in some areas.
6 We .... a 40% reduction in inventory.

| create | expand | exceed | rise | achieve | be |

Notice these sentences are in the present perfect tense. We use this tense to give news of recent events. For more information on the use of the present perfect, turn to page 160.

LANGUAGE WORK

Giving news   Graphic Images has just published its annual profit and loss account.

1   Match these explanations to the correct figures.

1   money paid to the shareholders
2   the cost of delivering goods to the customers
3   the money kept in the company and added to the reserves
4   the cost of managing the company
5   the cost of raw materials and manufacturing

Graphic Images PLC

CONSOLIDATED PROFIT AND LOSS ACCOUNT

	THIS YEAR **£m**	LAST YEAR £m
HOME SALES	189	175
EXPORT SALES	181	191
TOTAL SALES	370	366
COST OF SALES	(254)	(255)
GROSS PROFIT	116	111
DISTRIBUTION COSTS	(17)	(17)
ADMINISTRATIVE COSTS	(35)	(30)
PROFIT BEFORE TAX	64	64
TAX	(23)	(22)
PROFIT AFTER TAX	41	42
DIVIDEND	(36)	(34)
RETAINED PROFIT	5	8

2   Work with a colleague. Ask and answer questions about the figures.

A   *What's happened to sales this year?*
B   *They've* | *increased.*
          gone up.
          risen.

A   *What about profit after tax?*
B   *It's* | *decreased.*
        gone down.
        fallen.

A   *What about profit before tax?*
B   *It hasn't changed.*

3 Complete this year's Chairman's review. Put the verbs in brackets into the present perfect tense.

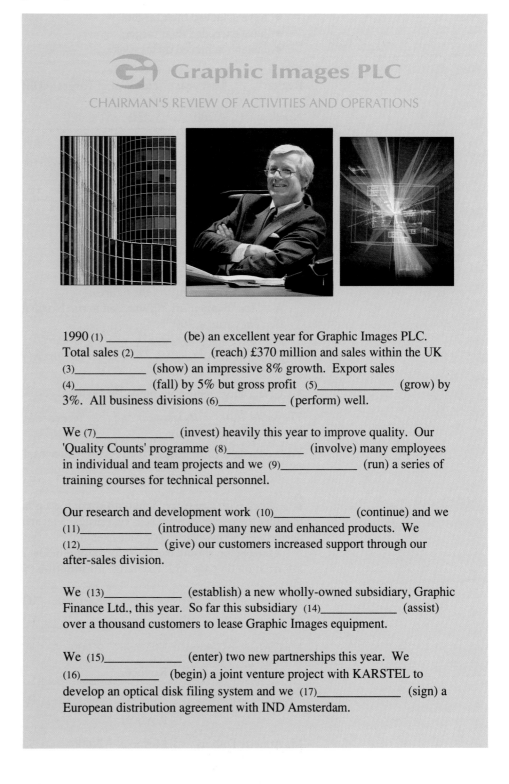

Graphic Images PLC

CHAIRMAN'S REVIEW OF ACTIVITIES AND OPERATIONS

1990 (1) _____ (be) an excellent year for Graphic Images PLC. Total sales (2)_____ (reach) £370 million and sales within the UK (3)_____ (show) an impressive 8% growth. Export sales (4)_____ (fall) by 5% but gross profit (5)_____ (grow) by 3%. All business divisions (6)_____ (perform) well.

We (7)_____ (invest) heavily this year to improve quality. Our 'Quality Counts' programme (8)_____ (involve) many employees in individual and team projects and we (9)_____ (run) a series of training courses for technical personnel.

Our research and development work (10)_____ (continue) and we (11)_____ (introduce) many new and enhanced products. We (12)_____ (give) our customers increased support through our after-sales division.

We (13)_____ (establish) a new wholly-owned subsidiary, Graphic Finance Ltd., this year. So far this subsidiary (14)_____ (assist) over a thousand customers to lease Graphic Images equipment.

We (15)_____ (enter) two new partnerships this year. We (16)_____ (begin) a joint venture project with KARSTEL to develop an optical disk filing system and we (17)_____ (sign) a European distribution agreement with IND Amsterdam.

4 What about your company's recent activities and operations? Write down six things your company or department has done recently and tell a colleague about them.

Targets

1   You are reviewing this year's regional sales results.

1   Which regions
   - have achieved their target?
   - have exceeded their target?
   - haven't achieved their target?

Region	Last year	This year	Target	Difference (%)
North	4,200	5,250	6,000	−12.5
South	5,400	7,300	7,000	+4.3
North-East	4,100	5,500	5,500	0
Midlands	2,950	4,250	4,000	+6.25
East	5,400	6,850	7,000	−2.1
South-West	2,950	4,600	4,600	0
South-East	4,100	5,650	5,800	−2.6

2   Question a colleague on the figures.
   A   *How many units did they sell in the North last year?*
   B   *They sold 4,200.*
   A   *And how many have they sold this year?*
   B   *They've sold 5,250. They haven't achieved the target.*

3   Give a short report on one of the regions.

They sold 4,200 units last year and they've exceeded that figure this year but they haven't achieved the target.

Your colleague must guess which region you are talking about.

2   Work with a partner. You both work for a pharmaceutical company. Each member of your sales team sells two drugs: Mevacin and Rovocor. You must decide who is this year's 'Top Sales Person'.
   One person should use the information below and the other should use the information on page 155. Exchange information to reach a decision.

		Last year	This year	Target	Difference (%)
Ms Catherine Ceretta	Mevacin	2,900	4,100	4,250	−3.6
	Rovocor				
Mr Philip Jacobsen	Mevacin	4,850	6,150	6,000	+2.5
	Rovocor				
Ms Annette Dubois	Mevacin	2,600	3,950	3,500	+12.8
	Rovocor				
Mr Peter Vogel	Mevacin	3,950	3,900	5,000	−22
	Rovocor				

Staffing levels

1 An insurance company has restructured its operations and moved a division from Royston to Harrow. Study the figures and complete the report below. Use the words in the box.

ROYSTON *Reductions in staffing levels*		HARROW *Increases in staffing levels*	
Natural Wastage			
Resigned	12	Employees transferring	30
Retired	4	New employees	25
Early Retirement	8	YTS recruits	10
Other Reductions			
Redundancies	28		
Transferred	30		
Dismissed	—		
Total Reduction	80	Total Increase	60
Target Reduction	80	Target Increase	80

The Claims Division has now moved to Harrow and we have achieved the target reductions in (1) .... at Royston. As far as possible, we have reduced the workforce by (2) .... ; we have not replaced workers who (3) .... for personal reasons or (4) .... at the age of 60. Some workers chose to (5) .... at 50 or 55 when we offered generous financial incentives. Many workers have (6) .... to the Harrow office.

One newspaper reported that we (7) .... or (8) .... four workers in Royston for misconduct. This was untrue. We have not (9) .... any workers this year. We have (10) .... 28 (11) .... in Royston but we have (12) .... 25 new staff in Harrow. We have also (13) .... 10 school leavers on the government's Youth Training Scheme.

dismissed	recruited	made staff redundant	taken on
resigned	retired	staffing levels	take early retirement
sacked	transferred	natural wastage	fired

2 Question a colleague about the figures.
Ask about the employees.
How many workers have resigned?

And ask about the company.
How many staff have they made redundant?

SKILLS WORK

Listening   You are going to listen to a recording of the business news. The radio announcer speaks quite fast and you won't be able to hear every word he says. These exercises will help you to pick out the important information.

1 Listening for the general meaning

Listen to the news without stopping the tape. Try to understand what each item is about. Listen again and write down two or three important words from each item. Compare your words with your colleagues'.

2 Listening for specific information

Listen to each item again and this time try to pick out specific information.

Item 1
The company: (1) ....
Their present market share: (2) ....
Their market share objective: (3) ....
Their pre-tax profits: (4) ....

Item 2
Movement of the pound (£) ↑ or ↓   ? (5)
Value against the German Mark: (6) ....

Item 3
Conner Peripherals will open a new plant in (7) ....
It will manufacture (8) ....
The company will invest (9) .... over the next three years.
The investment will create (10) .... new jobs.

Item 4
(11) Who is Geoffrey Whalen?
(12) What has he attacked?
(13) Why?
(14) What has he asked the government to do?

Speaking: Investment performance

Work with a colleague. One person should use the information below and the other should use the information on page 155.

You have shares in these companies:

	Holding (no. of shares)	Last week's price (p)	Today's price (p)
Nitro Chemicals	500	186	
Forsythe Bank	500	246	
Webb Communications	1,000	167	
Bespoke Tailoring	1,500	427	
Rose Computers	2,000	174	
Pharmedico Drugs	2,500	466	

Telephone your broker and find out how they have performed this week. Note down today's price in the chart.

Discuss your portfolio with your broker. Decide which shares you should buy more of and which shares you should sell.

	Buy or sell?	Quantity
Nitro Chemicals		
Forsythe Bank		
Webb Communications		
Bespoke Tailoring		
Rose Computers		
Pharmedico Drugs		

This morning's headlines:

Forsythe Bank computer fraud: employee steals £5m

AIDS CURE BREAKTHROUGH AT PHARMEDICO

Bespoke tailoring wins Queen's Award for Industry

When you have finished, turn to page 156 for next week's share prices.

11
Comparing Alternatives

OBJECTIVE
to compare alternative courses of action

TASKS

to compare two possible sites for a new factory

to complete reports on the economic performance of different countries

to choose between different suppliers

to make decisions based on comparative numerical data

to read and discuss an article on management styles

PRESENTATION

An American company is going to build a factory in Europe. Two managers discuss the two locations on the shortlist. One is Brignoles, in the Var in Southern France, and the other is Irvine in North West Scotland.

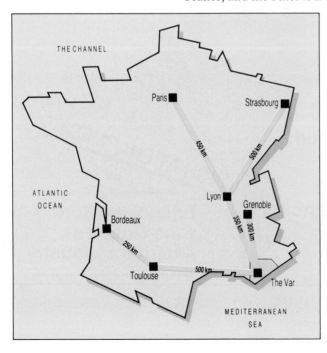

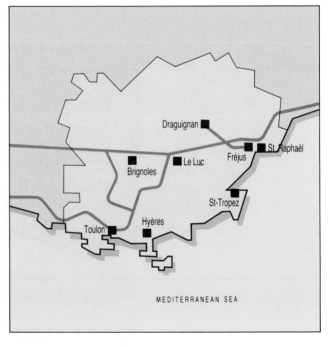

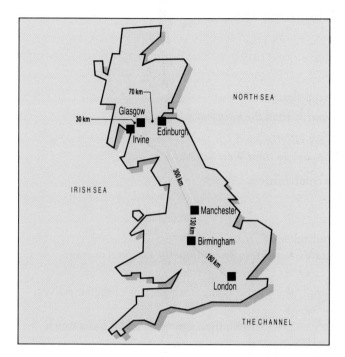

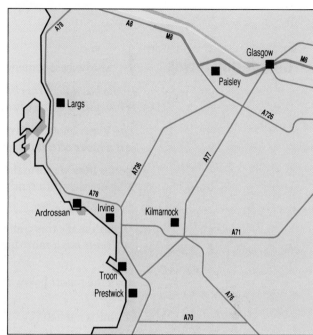

1 Before you listen, try to answer these questions.

1 Are labour costs lower in Brignoles or Irvine?
2 Are communications better in Brignoles or Irvine?
3 Is the climate nicer in Brignoles or Irvine?

Now listen to the dialogue and see if you were right.

2 Listen to the dialogue again and make a note of the advantages and disadvantages of each site.

	Advantages	**Disadvantages**
Brignoles (France)		
Irvine (Scotland)		

3 Supply the missing words in these sentences. One word per space.

1 Generally speaking, wages .... in Brignoles .... Irvine.

2 Irvine .... an international airport .... Brignoles.

3 France .... telecommunications system in Europe.

4 Climate .... important .... strategic location.

LANGUAGE WORK

Comparing towns

1 Study these sentences.

*Irvine has a **high** rate of unemployment.*
*It has a **higher** rate of employment **than** the national average.*

*The Var is an **attractive** region to live in.*
*It is a **more attractive** region to live in **than** West Scotland.*

Notice how we form the two comparatives.
Why are they different?

> Don't make this common mistake:
> **Irvine has a **more higher** rate of unemployment **than** the national average.*

Read the report below and supply the correct comparative forms of the adjectives.

> Irvine is a much (1) .... town than Brignoles and it has a much
> (big)
> (2) .... working population. Both towns have a
> (large)
> (3) .... rate of unemployment than the national average, but the
> (high)
> problem is much (4) .... in Irvine. Unemployment exceeds 20%
> (bad)
> and wages are generally (5) .... The Var has a
> (low)
> (6) .... number of skilled workers in the population.
> (great)
>
> Both towns offer financial incentives to attract businesses to the region. Irvine
> offers a (7) .... variety of loans at (8) ....
> (wide)   (competitive)
> interest rates but Brignoles offers (9) .... tax incentives. Factory
> (good)
> space is slightly (10) .... in Brignoles but consumer goods are
> (cheap)
> (11) ....
> (expensive)
>
> The Var is a (12) .... region to live in than West Scotland. The
> (attractive)
> climate is (13) .... and it will be (14) .... to attract and
> (warm)   (easy)
> keep well qualified staff. Communications will be a problem though. Brignoles
> is much (15) .... from an international airport than Irvine.
> (far)
>
> At present our main customers are in Northern Europe so Irvine is
> (16) .... and (17) .... But looking ahead, we
> (near)   (convenient)
> shouldn't forget that Brignoles is (18) .... to Spain,
> (close)
> Switzerland, and Italy, our next export targets.

2   Discuss the towns with two colleagues. Make comparisons using the table below.

A   *The climate is worse in Irvine.*
B   *That's true. The climate is much better in Brignoles.*
C   *Yes. The climate in Irvine isn't as good as the climate in Brignoles.*

	Irvine	Brignoles
Climate	bad	good
Working population	large	small
Rate of unemployment	high	low
Rates of pay	low	high
Skilled staff	difficult to find	easy to find
Factory space	expensive	cheap
An international airport	near	far

3   Which site should they choose: Brignoles or Irvine? Why?

Comparing countries

1   Your company is going to build three new factories around the world and you are collecting statistics. Study the graphs and complete the reports. Use only one word per space.

1   .... has the highest level of productivity.
.... has a higher level than Japan but a lower level than
Germany. .... has the lowest level of productivity.

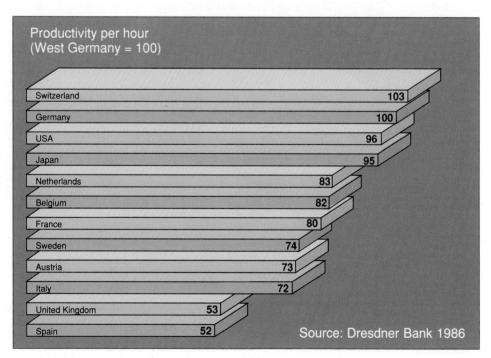

Productivity per hour
(West Germany = 100)

Switzerland	103
Germany	100
USA	96
Japan	95
Netherlands	83
Belgium	82
France	80
Sweden	74
Austria	73
Italy	72
United Kingdom	53
Spain	52

Source: Dresdner Bank 1986

2   Portugal has .... level of labour costs and
Switzerland has .... Spain has a
.... level .... Greece, but a
.... level .... Italy.

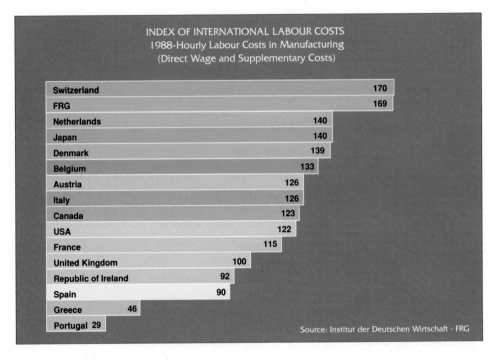

INDEX OF INTERNATIONAL LABOUR COSTS
1988-Hourly Labour Costs in Manufacturing
(Direct Wage and Supplementary Costs)

Country	Index
Switzerland	170
FRG	169
Netherlands	140
Japan	140
Denmark	139
Belgium	133
Austria	126
Italy	126
Canada	123
USA	122
France	115
United Kingdom	100
Republic of Ireland	92
Spain	90
Greece	46
Portugal	29

Source: Institut der Deutschen Wirtschaft - FRG

3   .... spends the most money on research and development.
.... spends less than Japan but more than France, and
.... spends the least.

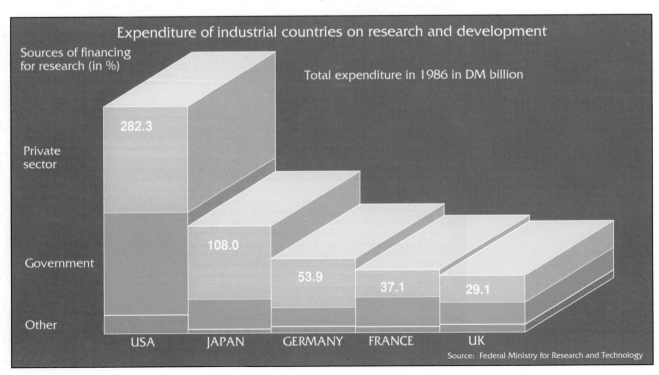

Expenditure of industrial countries on research and development

Sources of financing
for research (in %)

Total expenditure in 1986 in DM billion

Private
sector

Government

Other

USA	JAPAN	GERMANY	FRANCE	UK
282.3	108.0	53.9	37.1	29.1

Source: Federal Ministry for Research and Technology

4 Norwegians pay .... tax and Turks pay
.... The Japanese pay
.... the Italians but ....
.... the Austrians.

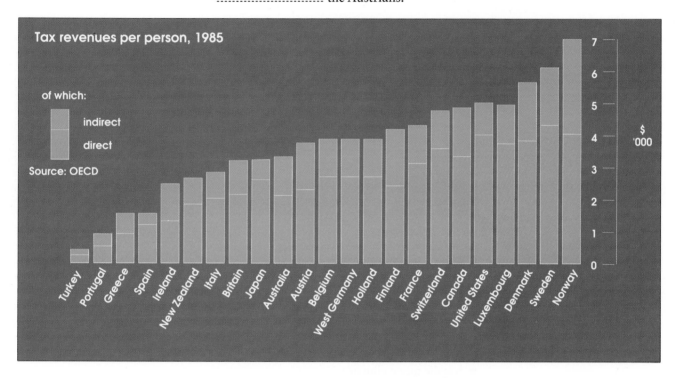

5 There are fewer students in full-time education in .... than in
Belgium, but there are more than in the Netherlands. .... has
the most students in higher education and .... has the fewest.

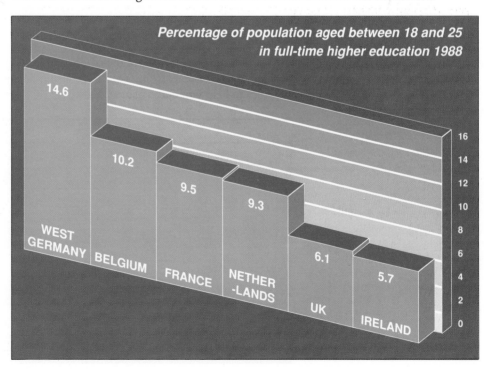

6   West Germany lost .... days through
    strikes and Belgium lost .... France lost
    .... the Netherlands but
    .... the UK.

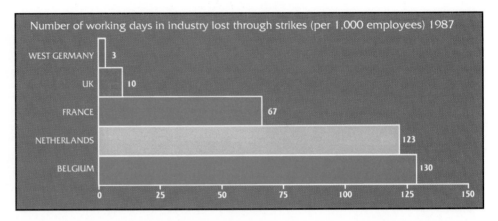

2   In your opinion, which country

- has the strongest economy?
- has the most growth potential?
- is the best country to build a new factory in?

And which country

- has the nicest climate?
- is the best country to visit for a holiday?
- is the best country to live in?

Why?

Comparing companies

1   Three companies produce the cardboard boxes you need. You are deciding which company to buy from. Your purchasing department has collected these statistics to help you make your minds up.

	EGP	THE CARD COMPANY	PAPER PACKS LTD
Price per standard 1 cubic metre box	7.56	7.4	7.83
No. of styles of boxes in the range	27	16	25
Quality – faults per 1,000 units	0.1	1.3	2.5
Delivery period	2 days	1 day	4 days
Discount	5%	10%	15%
Quantity kept in stock	100,000	600,000	500,000
Terms of payment	14 days	30 days	60 days

Work in pairs. Ask and answer the questions below.

Which company

1 has the highest/lowest prices?
2 has the widest/smallest product range?
3 has the best/worst quality record?
4 delivers the fastest/slowest?
5 gives the biggest/smallest discount?
6 keeps the most/fewest boxes in stock?
7 gives the most/least time to pay?

2 Cover up the questions. Look at the statistics and ask the questions again.

3 Which supplier is best? Why?

4 Tell a colleague about your company's competitors.

1 Who are your main competitors?
2 Which company working in your field
   • has the largest turnover?
   • employs the most people?
   • is the oldest?
   • has the most branches/locations/products?
   • provides the best service/product?

Why?

SKILLS WORK

Speaking **1** Work in small groups.
You all work for a US producer of chocolate confectionery. You are going to build your first production plant in Europe and you must decide where.

1 First, make some policy decisions. How important are the factors below?

2 Think of two more factors and add them to the list.

		Personal ranking	Group ranking
1	Low wage costs		
2	A strong economy		
3	An attractive environment and climate		
4	A good industrial relations record (i.e. not many strikes or labour disputes)		
5	A large home market		
6	A fast growing home market		
7	A central position in Europe		
8	Good rail, road and sea links with the rest of Europe		
9			
10			

Rank the factors in order of importance. Give 1 for the most important and 10 for the least important.

3 Compare your answers with your colleagues' and make a group ranking.

2 Now decide where to build your plant. This information will help you. (You can also use the graphs on pages 99–101.)

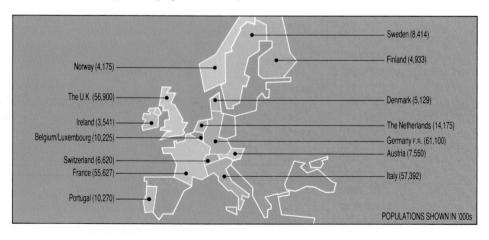

Norway (4,175)
The U.K. (56,900)
Ireland (3,541)
Belgium/Luxembourg (10,225)
Switzerland (6,620)
France (55,627)
Portugal (10,270)

Sweden (8,414)
Finland (4,933)
Denmark (5,129)
The Netherlands (14,175)
Germany F.R. (61,100)
Austria (7,550)
Italy (57,392)

POPULATIONS SHOWN IN '000s

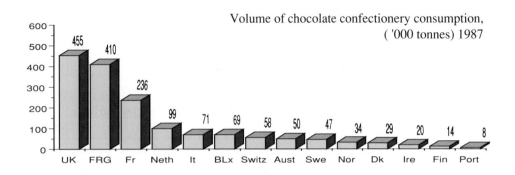

Volume of chocolate confectionery consumption, ('000 tonnes) 1987

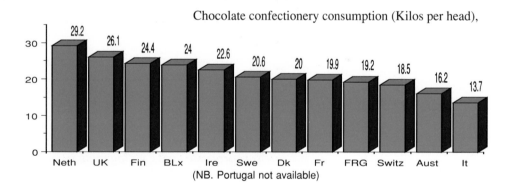

Growth in chocolate confectionery consumption, 1980–1987 (%)

(NB. Portugal not available)

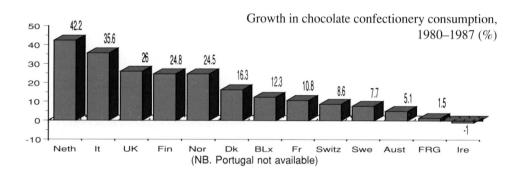

Chocolate confectionery consumption (Kilos per head),

(NB. Portugal not available)

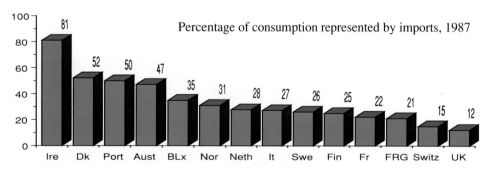

Percentage of consumption represented by imports, 1987

Source: IOCC

3 Make a short presentation to the class. Explain where you are going to locate your factory and why.

Reading

1 Do you agree or disagree with these statements?

		My opinion	Writer's opinion
1	People are naturally creative if you give them a chance.	Agree/Disagree	Agrees/Disagrees
2	Managers should tell workers what to do and how to do it.	Agree/Disagree	Agrees/Disagrees
3	People working at all levels of an organization should meet regularly to exchange information and plan improvements.	Agree/Disagree	Agrees/Disagrees
4	Companies need a centralized management to make decisions.	Agree/Disagree	Agrees/Disagrees
5	Employees prefer it when the management make all the decisions and they don't have a lot of responsibility.	Agree/Disagree	Agrees/Disagrees

2 Now read the article and decide if the writer agrees or disagrees with them.

More organizations are finding that employees at all levels can be a source of innovative and profitable ideas.

Participatory management, management by objectives, management by teams, quality circles – whatever you want to call it - is changing the traditional ways of management.

In brief, the philosophy is that you set free the natural creativity of people at all levels of the organization by encouraging them to set corporate goals, giving them what they need, and then leaving them alone to do the job.

The fuel that makes all this work is team spirit. Teams are formed vertically and horizontally so that all parts of the organization participate in sharing information and planning improvements.

Traditional authoritarian management disappears. In its place is decentralization and authority and responsibility placed at the lowest possible level.

For the organization, the results will be new ideas for products and services, better and more effective methods of working, and greater productivity at less cost.

For the employees, the benefits are greater self-fulfilment, a chance to progress, and a happier and smoother - running workplace.

3 *We place authority at the lowest level.*
We don't have an authoritarian style of management.

Authority is a noun or thing. *Authoritarian* is an adjective. It describes a noun.

Look for words in the article to complete the table below.

Noun	Adjective
authority	authoritarian
innovation	
profit	
tradition	
	creative
corporation	
	responsible
	productive
	beneficial

4 Choose an adjective or noun from the table to complete each of these sentences.

1 He's going to change the system completely with his fresh, new, i............................... ideas.
2 After-sales made a loss last year but they're going to make a small p............................... this year.
3 He prefers to do things in the old t............................... way.
4 We need to look for a c............................... solution to this problem.
5 The c............................... bosses met to discuss the takeover.
6 The salary is low for such a r............................... position.
7 Automation of the plant has resulted in greater p.............................. .
8 Management by objectives is b............................... to the company as a whole and the individuals who work in it.

5 Discuss the statements below.

1 People are naturally lazy. Managers should tell workers what to do or they won't do it.

2 Managers are paid a lot of money to make difficult decisions. They should make them themselves. They shouldn't ask their workers to make them for them.

3 An organization should have a central management structure so people's responsibilities are clear. If it doesn't, there will be chaos.

12

Planning Ahead

OBJECTIVE

to discuss future work plans and schedules

TASKS

to talk about quantity: *how much* and *how many*

to predict events in your company's future

to give strong advice to colleagues

to follow a briefing on a project schedule

to plan a new business venture

PRESENTATION

1 Two managers discuss the security arrangements for their company's new warehouse and distribution centre.

Listen to their conversation and decide which parts of the building they are talking about. Mark the appropriate dialogue number on the plan opposite.

2 Now listen again. Answer the questions and fill in the spaces. Use one word per space.

Dialogue 1
How many windows will there be?

----------- ----------- ----------- ----------- in here?
----------- ----------- ----------- only one door?

Dialogue 2
What will the gatehouse workers do?

----------- ----------- ----------- will work here?
----------- ----------- ----------- will they need?

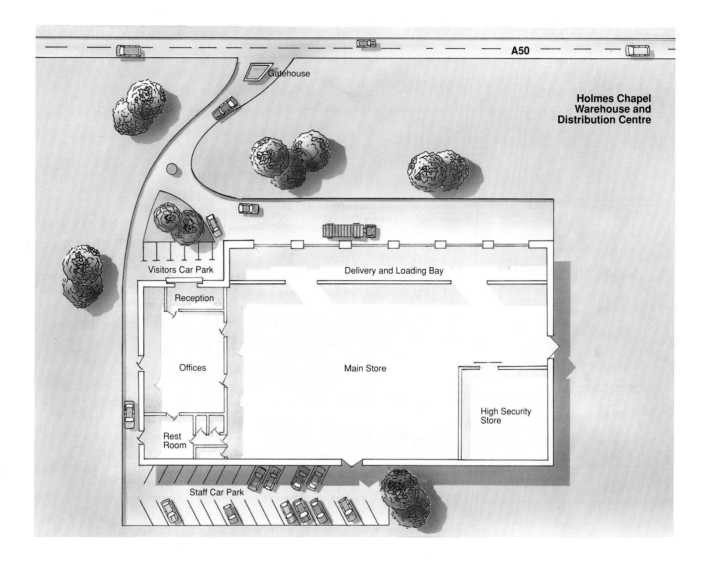

Dialogue 3

What will visitors do?

There .... space, ... ?
There .... visitors.

Dialogue 4

Why will security be a problem?

This area .... very busy.
Security .... a problem.

Dialogue 5

Why are the doors a problem?

.... have those doors there.
.... move the doors.

LANGUAGE WORK

Talking about quantity

1   A company is planning to build a new warehouse in Holmes Chapel. Read the briefing notes and list the advantages and disadvantages of the Holmes Chapel site.

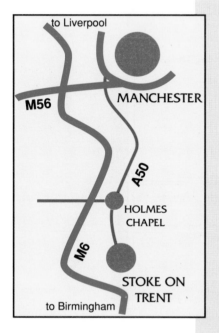

HOLMES CHAPEL WAREHOUSE AND DISTRIBUTION CENTRE

BRIEFING NOTES

STRATEGIC LOCATION

Holmes Chapel is situated on the A50, one mile from the M6 motorway. Located in the centre of England, it is only 45 minutes from Manchester, 60 minutes from Liverpool, 70 minutes from Birmingham, and three and a half hours from London. The town has a higher than average level of rainfall but snow is unusual and we do not expect bad winters to affect communications.

THE TOWN

The town of Holmes Chapel has a population of 6,000. There are two factories producing wallpaper and chemicals and a few small light industrial units. It is not in an enterprise zone and there are no government subsidies available. The unemployment rate is low. There are a large number of farms around the town and agriculture is the main employer in the area.

THE SITE

The 2.5 hectare site provides plenty of space for the development. At present it is completely undeveloped with no mains services. We plan to lay pipes for gas, electricity, and water before we begin Phase 1 of the development in July.

2   Complete these sentences about Holmes Chapel using words from the box.

There's a lot of (1) ....
There are a lot of (2) ....

There isn't much (3) ....
There aren't many (4) ....

There isn't any (5) ....
There aren't any (6) ....

rain	unemployment
snow	farms
people living in Holmes Chapel	agricultural workers
factories	space for the development
heavy industry	buildings on the site
government subsidies	gas or electricity on the site

3   Describe your home town in the same way. Make sentences beginning *There is/isn't* . . . or *There are/aren't* . . . .

4   Find out about a colleague's home town. Ask questions beginning *Is there much* . . .? or *Are there many* . . .? Ask about the points below.

1	industry	5	parks	8	golf courses
2	unemployment	6	old buildings	9	restaurants
3	immigrants	7	snow	10	nightlife
4	open space				

5   Are these nouns countable (C), uncountable (U) or both (U:C)?

☐ information   ☐ money   ☐ scientist   ☐ job

☐ fact   ☐ dollar ($)   ☐ people   ☐ work

☐ suggestion   ☐ machinery   ☐ staff   ☐ time

☐ advice   ☐ machine   ☐ paper

☐ help   ☐ equipment   ☐ newspaper

6   Complete these sentences. Use *much* with uncountable nouns and *many* with countable nouns.

1   There aren't .... staff in that department.
2   How .... equipment do you need?
3   I'm afraid I can't give you .... information about that.
4   We didn't buy .... paper last month.
5   There aren't .... machines working today.
6   We haven't got .... money left.
7   How .... yen are there to the dollar?
8   He made some suggestions but he didn't offer .... help.
9   How .... people were there at the meeting?
10   Are there .... jobs left to do?
11   I haven't done ....work today.
12   .... scientists disagree with that theory.
13   How .... times have you been to England?
14   How .... time can I spend on this project?

Predicting the future   **1**   We often use *will* to make predictions about the future.
Security will be a problem.
There won't be much space.

Are these predictions true for your company?

1	Our turnover will increase.	7	We'll introduce new technology.
2	The company will expand.	8	Our staff will need more training.
3	Our market share will rise.	9	There will be a shortage of good staff.
4	Competition from abroad will increase.	10	We will reduce the workforce.
5	We will go out of business.	11	Prices of raw materials will rise.
6	Demand for our products will rise.	12	Our prices will fall.

Compare answers with your colleagues.

2 What is this advertisement for?

Act out the conversation with a partner. These phrases will help you.

We'll need . . .   *Will we need . . . ?*
We'll want . . .   *Will we want . . . ?*

Giving advice

We use *You'd better* to give strong advice, for example:

A *I've received some faulty parts from one of our suppliers.*
B *You'd better not accept them. You'd better send them back.*

Work with one or two colleagues. Take it in turns to give each other advice. Say *You'd better . . .* and *You'd better not . . .*

1 There's a mistake on this invoice.
2 They want me to sign a contract but I don't understand the small print.
3 I've received a bad reference for one of the candidates for the new sales job.
4 I'm planning to go on holiday next week but four of my staff are off sick.
5 I have to give a presentation in five minutes and I can't find my notes.
6 My English isn't good enough to negotiate the deal and the translator hasn't arrived.

SKILLS WORK

Listening **1** A manager explains the schedule for a construction project.

1 Listen to Part One. When will these events happen?

	When?
The distribution operations will move to Holmes Chapel.	
The Melbourne Street site will become vacant.	
Construction work will begin.	
They will complete Phase 1.	
They will establish a schedule for Phase 2.	

2 Listen again and supply the missing words in these sentences.

a We .... move our distribution operations . . .
b We .... take this opportunity . . .
c We .... complete phase 1 in 18 months.
d We .... establish the schedule next month.

3 What other future plans has the company got?
Look at the information below. Say what they *plan*, *intend*, *aim* and *hope* to do, for example:

They are looking for a distributor in Eastern Europe.
They plan to start exporting to Eastern Europe.

a They are looking for a distributor in Eastern Europe.
b They have increased the research and development budget.
c Their sales office in Qatar loses a lot of money every year.
d Their internal telephone system is out of date.
e They are looking for a joint venture partner with experience in launching satellites.
f They are buying robots.
g They have set high sales targets.

4 Write about your company's future plans. Complete these sentences.

We plan to ....
We intend to ....
We aim to ....
We hope to ....

2 1 Listen to Part Two. What jobs will everyone have?

- What will the committee do?
- What will the working groups do?
- What will the project manager do?

2 How often will the committee meet the property developers? How often will the project manager organize a newsletter?

Supply the missing words in the gaps below.

(every three months)		a *quarterly*	newsletter
(every week)		a	magazine
(every month)		a	bulletin
(every day)		a	paper
(every hour)		an	update
(every year)		a	report
	or	an	report

Speaking

Work in a small group with two or three colleagues.

1 You have decided to leave your present jobs and set up in business together. Plan the venture.

1 What sort of business will you set up?
Service (What service will you offer?)
or manufacturing? (What will you produce?)
What competitors will you have?
How will your product/service be different from theirs?

2 Consider the talents and skills of everyone in the group.
What jobs will you all do in the new organization?

3 What premises (building/offices) will you need?
What equipment will you need?
What machinery will you need?
What staff will you need?

4 How will you advertise your product/service?

5 How much capital (start-up money) will you need?
How will you finance your operations?

6 When will you start the venture? Prepare a schedule.

2 Report back to the class. Tell them your plans. They must ask questions and give advice.

13

Business Travel

PRESENTATION

1 Did you have any problems travelling on your last trip abroad? What were they?

let me in / dejame entrar
let me out. salir

2 Listen to three conversations at an airport. For each one, note down the traveller's problem and destination.

Dialogue 1
Problem ..... *his visa expired / nsited to US.*
the immigration Authorities

Destination ..... *New York*

Immigration Authorities

Dialogue 2
Problem ..... *she is alergic to smok.*
She has to take an other flyght
the airline pass the bagage to an

Destination ..... *another plain*
NEW CASTLE
What about my bagage

Dialogue 3
Problem .....
..... *economy class*

Destination ..... *Paris*

9:45

where can I pick up my logage
claim my logage o bagage

116

3   Listen to Dialogue 1 again and supply the missing words below. One word per space.

1   _____ *Can I* _____ get one in New York?
2   No _____ *You have* _____ apply from outside the USA.
3   So _____ *I can* _____ get on this flight?

What will happen if the traveller goes to New York?

the

4   Listen to Dialogue 2 again. What mustn't the traveller do? Why not? What <u>doesn't she have to do</u>? Why not?

algo ql no es necesario
ause to veable to

5   Listen to dialogue 3 again and supply the missing words below.

1   If there's a seat in economy, _____ *gave* _____ *me* _____ *overbook*
    _____ *that* _____.
2   I'll see if _____ *there's* _____ *a* _____ *seat* _____.
3   What happens if _____ *the* _____ *resons* _____?
4   We'll get you a seat with another airline if _____ *we* _____
    _____ *have* _____ *to* _____.

6   Act out the last conversation with a partner. These words will help your memory.

vuelo lleno

A afraid / overbooked	B last week
A very sorry /	B must / Paris / ten o'clock
	B if / seat in economy / give me that
A afraid whole plane / full next flight / 9.35 / too late?	
A I'll see / seat	B No
A seat with another airline / have to	B What happens / if not?

chekin

117

LANGUAGE WORK

Air travel

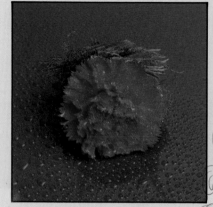

10 "I have to ring my office."

5 "What's the taxi fare to the city centre?"

1 "Who won last night's ball game?"

8 "What's the code for Cleveland, Ohio?"

1 "Is it too early for the bar?"

7 "I have to be in Alaska by 8 tonight."

6 "Can I go through to the Departure Lounge now?"

2 "Is there anybody here to meet Mrs Leroy?"

3 "Where can I get a bus into town?"

9 "I can't find my boarding card."

"Do they take travellers' cheques at 3 the Duty Free?"

7 "Where's the Gents?"

4 "How long is the stopover?"

8 "Will the flight leave on time?"

9 "Am I in time?"

1 "What star sign is the pilot?"

2 "I can't find a porter."

6 "Where are all the trolleys?"

5 "Can I leave my luggage here overnight?"

10 "Is this ticket out of date?"

8 Where do I check in?" 7

"Where can I rent a car?" 10

"Can I reserve a hotel room in Denver, Colorado?"

"Which gate are we boarding from?"

"I have to catch the shuttle at 7." 6

"Do I have to declare my camera?"

"What's going on?" 9

5 "Can you cancel my hotel reservation?"

3 "I think that's my plane taking off."

10 "Please, somebody."

TWA have the answers.

We listened to travellers' questions at the airport and came up with an answer, in fact we came up with lots of answers - the TWA 'White Coats'.
'White Coats' are a team of young men and women at our Heathrow and JFK terminals - all available to help with your problems.
So the next time you're waiting for one of our six daily flights to the USA and your passport disappears or your colleague needs some elastic in a hurry, speak to the person in the white jacket with a red carnation in the buttonhole.

UP TO 9
el maximo es 9.

1 Which airline is this advertisement for?
What special service are they advertising?

2 Look at the left-hand column in the advertisement. Match the replies below
to the correct problem.

1   No, it opened 10 minutes ago.
2   No, but we've got a message for you.
3   There's an airport limousine downstairs.
4   The Cincinatti Reds.
5   Around £50.
6   Certainly. Go ahead.
7   I'll look up the best connection. *lunch*
8   010 1 216.
9   When did you last have it?
10   There's a phone over there.

3 Look at the centre column in the advertisement. Find words or phrases that mean

1   a person who flies planes
2   a person who carries luggage
3   a tax-free shop
4   a short stay in a place between connecting flights
5   baggage
6   things to carry baggage
7   the men's toilet
8   at the correct time
9   not late
10   expired (no longer useful or valid).

4 Look at the right-hand column in the advertisement. Find verbs or phrases
that mean

1   getting on a plane *avanzar*
2   to tell a customs officer about something you are carrying *cargando loque lleva mi maleta.*
3   leaving the ground (a plane)
4   to book
5   the opposite of *to book*
6   the opposite of *to miss*   *Land = Aterrizar*
7   to hire
8   to register for a flight
9   happening
10   help!

5 Work with a partner. Take it in turns to be travellers asking the questions
and a 'White Coat' answering them.

AT = en un lugar General No tan... especifico
On = on the first floor.

Rules and regulations

1 Study the table below then use each verb once to complete the regulations.

can	possible
can't/cannot	impossible
must	necessary or
have to	obligatory
don't have to	not necessary
mustn't	prohibited or forbidden

1 Passengers _have to_ make sure their luggage is clearly labelled.
2 Passengers _don't have to_ take a small bag onto the plane with them.
3 Passengers _can't_ carry dangerous articles such as compressed gases, weapons, explosives, or fireworks.
4 Passengers _must_ check in 60 minutes before departure on international flights.
5 Passengers _don't have to_ check in 60 minutes before departure on domestic flights, 30 minutes is sufficient.
6 The airline _can't_ accept responsibility for delays due to bad weather.

2 Notice the difference between *mustn't* and *don't have to*. Decide which to use in these sentences.

1 They transfer our baggage to the next plane. We _don't have to_ carry it.
2 Passengers _mustn't_ use radio telephones because they interfere with the planes' electronic equipment.
3 Passengers _mustn't_ smoke when the plane is taking off or landing.
4 You _don't have to_ take out travel insurance, but it's a good idea.
5 This meeting is very important. We _mustn't_ be late.
6 We've got plenty of time. You _don't have to_ hurry.
7 You _don't have to_ return the car to the place you hired it. You can return it to another Hertz garage.
8 If you haven't got an international licence, you _mustn't_ drive.
9 You _don't have to_ pay to drive on motorways in England.
10 We can buy a ticket at the station. We _don't have to_ book in advance.

3 Compare your company's regulations and systems with a partner. Talk about the topics below. (Work with someone from a different organization if you can.)

travel expenses	holidays	smoking	sickness	security
retirement	lunch breaks	company cars	safety	

Make sentences beginning:

We can . . .	*We must . . .*	*We mustn't . . .*
We can't . . .	*We have to . . .*	*We don't have to . . .*

Future possibilities

1 Match the two halves of these sentences.

1 If she bought a discount ticket, _d_ .
2 If I can't get a flight home, _l_
3 If it's 11 a.m. in London, _k_
4 If they've caught the 2.30 from Paddington, _i_
5 If you haven't got anything to declare, _h_
6 If you're travelling to Mozambique, _a_
7 If the sea is rough, _b_ *picado* *terrible, espero*
8 If you keep the receipts, _c_ *recibo*
9 If you're travelling from London to New York, _j_
10 If you have to be there by ten, _f_
11 If you haven't met before, _e_
12 If she wasn't on that flight, _g_ .

a) you must have a typhoid innoculation.
b) there are no hovercraft flights.
c) we'll refund your travel expenses.
d) she won't be able to change it.
e) how will you recognize him at the airport?
f) you'd better hurry up. *(mejor te apuran)*
g) she'll be on the next one. → *A travez de*
h) go through the green door.
i) they'll be here in half an hour.
j) put your watch back five hours.
k) it's 8 p.m. in Tokyo.
l) I'll have to stay overnight. → *toda la noche* *pasar la noche*

For more information on conditionals see page 164.

2 You are going on a very important business trip to negotiate a large contract with a new supplier.

abroad = Extranjero
New supplier = Proveedor
Supply = Provisionen

What will you do if

- you miss your flight?
- you lose your luggage?
- your supplier is ill?
- your supplier can't speak English?
- your supplier speaks English, but too quickly?
- your supplier invites you to lunch?
- your supplier's price is too high?
- your supplier offers you a bribe? → *soborno* *mordida*

MISS =
hire a translater.

| *If I miss my flight,* | *I'll catch the next one.* |
| | *I'll have to phone my supplier and explain.* |

3 A client/colleague/customer from abroad is visiting you at your place of work next week. You are not sure how long they are staying or what they want to see. Write down some possible things to do. Think of

- people they could meet
- a guided tour of . . .
- processes to show them
- somewhere to have lunch
- a presentation by . . . on . . .
- a presentation video/slide show
- a place to have lunch
- an interesting place to visit nearby.

Work with a colleague. Take it in turns to be the visitor. The host(ess) should explain the different possibilities and find out what the visitor wants to do.

If you like,	*we can . . .*
If there's time,	*we could . . .*
If you're interested,	*we'll . . .*
If the weather's OK,	
If . . .	

121

SKILLS WORK

Speaking 1

1 Your company is reviewing its policies for business travel arrangements and expenses. Study the proposals below.
What will happen if you implement them?

If staff travel economy class on flights, we can save a lot of money.
If staff have to travel economy class, they won't like it.

Graphic Images PLC

PROPOSALS

1 Staff should travel economy class instead of business class on flights.

2 We should stop paying for alcoholic drinks at business lunches.

3 We should have a car pool instead of providing individual staff members with cars.

4 We should lease the company cars instead of buying them.

5 We should only buy/lease small cars (maximum engine size - 1,000 cc).

6 We should install meters in the company car park.

2 Hold a meeting to discuss the proposals. Decide which proposals to implement.

Speaking 2

Think of some changes you would like to make to a system at work. Imagine changes to

- methods of work
- communications procedures
- production systems
- the products/services that you provide
- your premises (the buildings you operate in)
- methods of supply
- methods of distribution
- any other process or arrangement that you can think of.

Argue the case for introducing changes.

1 Outline the present system or arrangement.
2 Explain the changes you want to make.
3 Explain why you want to make the changes. (What will happen if you do/don't?).
4 Answer questions from your colleagues.

122

2 Now listen again and answer these questions.

1 What is AMP's annual growth rate?
How long have they had this growth rate?

2 How much do they spend on research and development?
How long have they been doing this?

3 What do they produce?
How long have they been in business?

LANGUAGE WORK

Corporate development

THE AMP CORPORATION	
1941	A. U. Whitaker founded AMP.
1943	Invented the pre-insulated terminal that gave the company long-term leadership in the market.
1952	Set up the first foreign subsidiaries in Puerto Rico, France, and Canada.
1959	Went public*.
1966	Joined the *Fortune* Magazine list of America's 500 largest corporations.
1983	Opened a new corporate headquarters in Harrisburg, Pennsylvania.
1988	Acquired Matrix Science Corporation.

*The company's stock/shares were listed on the New York Stock Exchange.

1 Work with a partner. Ask and answer questions about AMP's past.

A *When* | *did Whitaker found AMP?*
How long ago |
B *In 1941.*
About 50 years ago.

2 All these actions happened in the past, but they connect to the present. For example, AMP still produce the pre-insulated terminal and they still have subsidiaries abroad.

Work with a partner. Ask and answer questions about the present.

How long have AMP | *been in business?*
been producing the pre-insulated terminal?
had a subsidiary in Puerto Rico?
been a public listed company?
been in the Fortune *Magazine list?*
been operating from their new headquarters?
owned Matrix Science Corporation?

They've | *been in business since 1941.*
been producing the pre-insulated terminal since 1943.
had a subsidiary in Puerto Rico since 1952.
been a public listed company since 1959.
been in the Fortune *Magazine 500 list since 1966.*
been operating from their new headquarters since 1983.
owned Matrix Science Corporation since 1988.

Grammar note

The present perfect simple and continuous

Study these two forms of the present perfect.

They've been producing | *the pre-insulated terminals since 1943.*
They've produced |

In this situation the meaning is the same. English speakers usually use the continuous form, *They've been producing . . .*, but with verbs like *be* and *have*, this is not possible.
They've been in business since 1941.

A job advertisement

1 Would you like this job? Have you got the right qualifications and experience?

ASSISTANT DIRECTOR CORPORATE FINANCE

Our client is a highly successful subsidiary of a major US corporation at the leading edge of developments in laser technology. For the last four years they have been expanding their UK operations and are now looking for an experienced negotiator to spearhead their expansion into Europe.
You will be a graduate and ACA-qualified accountant with an impressive track record in an industrial company. You will have hands-on experience in contract negotiation and your responsibilities will include making cross-border deals, particularly with France, Germany, and southern Europe.
This challenging and demanding position will have a strong influence on our client's European performance. That's why you will need to be creative, imaginative and capable of working to tight deadlines.
In return you can expect generous financial rewards, exciting opportunities for achievement, and possibilities for further career development in a fast-growing, blue-chip company.
For more information, please write with full career details.

2 Look through the advertisement and find expressions that fit the explanations below.

1 in the front, where the exciting developments happen
2 to lead their expansion
3 a history of past success
4 practical experience, not theoretical
5 international deals
6 high payments, salary, etc.
7 a profitable company with a good reputation

3 Look through the advertisement again and make a list of words and phrases that describe
● the company
● the job
● the person they are looking for.

Do any of the words or phrases describe
● your company?
● your job?
● you?

Imagine you are writing an advertisement for your job. What information will you include?

Talking about experience

1 Joseph Towns is applying for the job of Assistant Director, Corporate Finance. Look at his career résumé. Has he got the right qualifications and experience?

Has he
- qualified as an accountant?
- been to university?
- ever worked for an industrial company?
- had experience of negotiating international deals?
- ever worked abroad?

CAREER RÉSUMÉ

NAME	Joseph Franklin Towns
NATIONALITY	British
EDUCATION	King's College, Cambridge (1981-84) BA Mathematics. 1st Class Honours.
PROFESSIONAL QUALIFICATIONS	ACA Institute of Chartered Accountants of England and Wales.
PREVIOUS POSITIONS	**ERNST & YOUNG, CHARTERED ACCOUNTANTS** (1984-89)

Auditor (Audit Section 1984-87)
Auditing Experience: Local Government Authorities, banks, petroleum and engineering companies.

Consultant (Business Advisory Section 1987-89)
Consultancy Experience: Negotiating takeovers, mergers, and management buyouts in PLCs and USM listed companies.

RKI CHEMICALS (1989-Present)

Financial Accountant
Corporate Experience: Negotiating international agency contracts and franchise agreements.

Transferred to Paris branch in 1991.

---

2 Use information from the career résumé to complete this table.

	Number of years
Ernst & Young	5
RKI Chemicals	
Auditor	
Financial Accountant	
Cambridge	
Paris	

3 Notice we use the past tense if the action is completed or finished.
He worked for Ernst & Young for five years.

And we use the present perfect tense if the action is still continuing.
He's been working for RKI Chemicals for five years.

Now work with a partner. Ask and answer questions about Joseph Towns's experience.

How long did he work for Ernst & Young?
How long has he been working for RKI Chemicals?

For more information on the present perfect tense turn to page 160.

4 Notice that we use *for* with a length of time and *since* with a point in time.

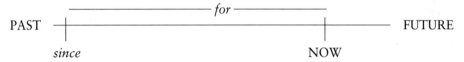

He's been working for RKI Chemicals **for** *five years.*
He's been working for RKI Chemicals **since** *1989.*

Decide whether to use *for* or *since* with the time expressions below.

1	2 days	5	last week	9	years
2	an hour	6	1945	10	yesterday
3	Wednesday	7	a month	11	the 1960s
4	a long time	8	2 o'clock	12	the stockmarket crash

5 Find out about your partner's work experience.

Ask
- who they work for (how long?)
- who they worked for before (how long?)
- what their job is (how long?)
- what their job was before (how long?)
- where they live (how long?)
- where they lived before (how long?).

Bad experiences

Have you ever wondered why you're doing your job? Everyone has to do things they don't like sometimes. Find out about some of the bad experiences your colleagues have had.

Ask the questions below. If the answer is *Yes, I have*, ask more questions, for example *When was that?*, *What happened?*, *What did you do?* (Notice that these questions are in the past tense. For more information on the use of the present perfect and past tenses, see page 160.)

Have you ever
- had to cancel a holiday because of pressure of work?
- been late for an important meeting?
- had to sack someone?
- missed the last flight home?
- had to make a difficult speech?
- had a trade journalist misquote you?
- had to be nice to a client you don't like?
- had to lie to a client?
- worked all through the night?
- had to wear a suit when the temperature's sky-high?
- had a big argument with your boss?
- had to defend a decision you disagreed with?
- thought about resigning and starting your own business?

SKILLS WORK

Speaking   Divide into two groups of equal size.

Group One
You are all managers who are thinking of changing your jobs. Some people from an executive recruitment agency will approach you. Answer their questions.

Group Two
You work for an executive recruitment agency. You are looking for good managers to fill top jobs.

Interview the people in the other group and collect information on the table below to add to your data base.

PROFESSIONAL RECRUITMENT

NAME	PRESENT JOB
COMPANY	LENGTH OF TIME IN JOB
EDUCATION & QUALIFICATIONS	EXPERIENCE
LANGUAGES	

PREVIOUS JOBS	LENGTH OF TIME

Writing   **1**   What is this advertisement for? Is it advertising a product? Which newspapers or magazines have advertisements like this?

BORAL LIMITED ONE OF AUSTRALIA'S FASTEST-GROWING COMPANIES

BORAL LIMITED. ONE OF AUSTRALIA'S FASTEST-GROWING COMPANIES

The Boral Group is a leading supplier to the building and construction industries, a major force in energy and resources and a powerful performer in manufacturing.

Boral has been growing rapidly since it began trading in 1948 and it is now one of Australia's largest and strongest companies. For the last twelve years the group has been expanding fast in the US, the Pacific Basin, Europe, and South East Asia so that today 22% of Boral's business activities are outside Australia.

Chairman Sir Peter Finley told the Annual General Meeting: 'The company is in a sound financial position with a strong balance sheet. We earn our profits from solid assets which are geographically well spread, and the company enjoys a strong cash flow.'

For investors the most important growth area has been profitability. Boral has recorded increases in profit for 19 successive years.

In 1988/89 sales of over $3,625 million resulted in a net profit after tax of $A301. Earnings per share were 42.2 cents.

BORAL

Copies of our annual report can be obtained from Boral Limited, Norwich House, 6-10 O'Connell Street, Sydney, Australia.

2 Complete this passage with information from the advertisement.

The Boral Group is a leading supplier to the (1) .... industries. Its business activities also include work in the areas of (2) .... and (3) .... and manufacturing. Boral has been in business for (4) .... years and has been (5) .... in the US, the Pacific Basin, Europe, and South East Asia for (6) .... Profits have increased for (7) .... successive years.

(8) .... are available from Boral Limited, Norwich House, 6–10 O'Connell Street, Sydney, Australia.

3 Use the advertisement and passage as a guide and write an advertisement for your company.

15

Systems and Processes

OBJECTIVE

to explain systems and processes in the workplace

TASKS

---

to follow a factory tour

---

to write a report on the benefits of a leasing system

---

to describe the sequence of events in a manufacturing process

---

to follow an explanation of a company's ordering system

---

to describe and explain a process in your workplace

PRESENTATION

1 Listen to a manager of a car assembly plant showing some visitors round. As you listen, number these photographs in the right order.

☐ Fitting the windscreen

☐ Testing the brakes

☐ Hanging the doors

☐ Fitting the mechanical components

☐ Testing the car on the track

☐ Constructing the car body

| Fitting the wheels | Painting the body | Constructing the chassis |

2 Now use the pictures to describe the process.

A *The car body is constructed.*
B *What happens* | *next?*
                     | *then?*
                     | *after that?*
A *The doors are hung.*

3 Read the sentences in columns A and B. Which steps in the car assembly process are they describing? Match them to a photograph.

A	B	Step number
We press the glass onto the windscreen opening.	The glass is pressed onto the windscreen opening.	☐
We use electronic sensors to position the doors.	The doors are positioned accurately by electronic sensors.	☐
We use a computer to test the brakes.	The brakes are tested by a sophisticated computer programme.	☐
We test the cars over different road conditions.	The cars are tested over different road conditions.	☐

4 How are the sentences in columns A and B different? Which are more

- formal?
- informal?
- likely to be spoken?
- likely to be written?
- technical?

What differences in grammar are there?

For more information on the passive voice turn to page 165.

135

LANGUAGE WORK

A leasing system

1 You are examining the possibility of leasing your company's fleet of lorries. Read this advertisement for Lex Van Contracts. Which services are the most useful?

Lex Van Contracts take away the headaches of running the company fleet and allow you to get on with running the business.

- We advise customers on the most cost-effective and efficient vehicles for their specific needs.
- We inspect every vehicle before delivery.
- We arrange signwriting.
- We replace tyres, batteries and exhausts when necessary.
- We service the vehicles at any time of the day or night.
- We provide a 24-hour recovery service.
- We deal with all the paperwork.
- We record the service history of our customers' fleets on our computer.

2 You decide to recommend Lex Van Contracts to your board. Write a report on all the services they offer. Use the passive voice in your report.

MEMORANDUM

Date: ....
To: *Helen Williams, General Manager*
From: ...., *Research Assistant*
Subject: *Fleet Leasing*...

As requested, I have been examining the possibility of leasing our fleet of lorries and I have found a suitable leasing company. Lex Van Contracts have an excellent reputation in the fleet leasing market. They provide a number of valuable services.

1 Customers, *are advised on the most cost-effective and efficient vehicles for their needs*.

2 Every vehicle_____

3 Signwriting_____

4 Tyres, batteries, and exhausts_____

5 The vehicles_____

6 A 24-hour recovery service_____

7 All the paperwork_____

8 The service history_____

These services will offer substantial savings of administrative time and money. I therefore recommend we invite Lex to run the company fleet.

Processes   **1**   Study the flow chart and complete the passage below, using the passive voice. Use one word per space.

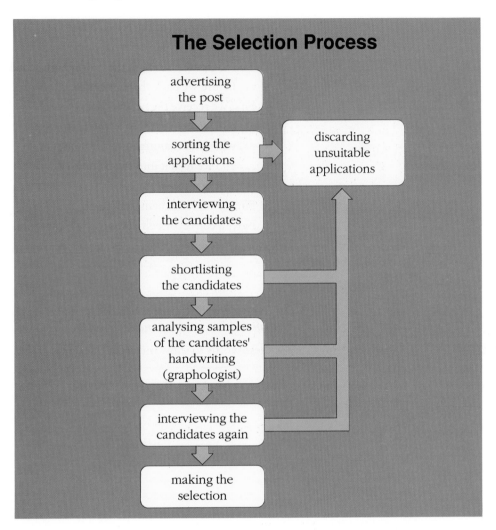

First the post (1) .... in the local or national press. When the applications arrive they (2) .... and unsuitable applications (3) .... Next the candidates (4) .... and (5) ....

Then samples of the best candidates' handwriting are sent to a graphologist where they (6) .... After that, the successful candidates (7) .... again, and finally the selection (8) ....

Notice these words

First   *Next*   *Finally*
            Then
            After that

They are useful for showing the order of events.

2 Look at a factory manager's description of the process of making car bumpers. The steps are in the wrong order. Number them in the correct order.

> We don't keep stocks of the finished bumpers. We operate a 'just in time' system.
>
> ☐ The computer arranges the production schedule.
> ☐ . . . before we pack them in crates.
> ☐ First we receive the order . . .
> ☐ . . . and we deliver them to the customers.
> ☐ . . . where we manufacture the bumpers.
> ☐ . . . and we feed it into the computer.
> ☐ We test the bumpers . . .
> ☐ Finally we load them into lorries . . .
> ☐ Next a conveyor belt takes the raw materials to the factory floor . . .
>
> The whole process only takes about nine hours from start to finish.

3 Now describe the process more formally, as shown below.
First an order is received and fed into . . .

Use these words to show the order of events.

First	*Next*	*before*	*Finally*

SKILLS WORK

Listening **1** What do you think this graph represents?

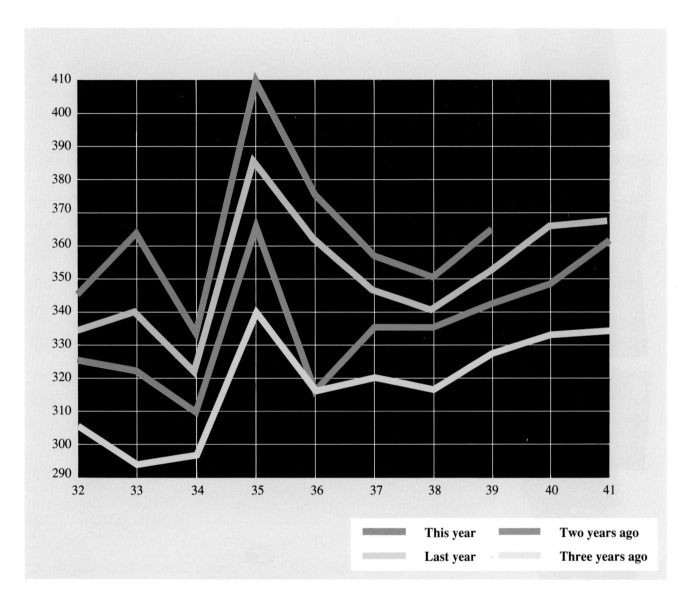

This year *Two years ago*
Last year *Three years ago*

2 Read this extract from the talk you are going to hear.

> We have to anticipate how many we're going to sell of each particular line. If we can anticipate the fact that a customer is going to want more next week we can make more. If we just look at last week's sales figures, we're reacting to what they wanted last week. We're not anticipating what they will want next week. We need to see the whole trading pattern to anticipate.

- What does *anticipate* mean?
- How is this extract connected with the graph?

3 Now listen to a bakery manager describing his production planning process. As you listen, complete the flow chart.

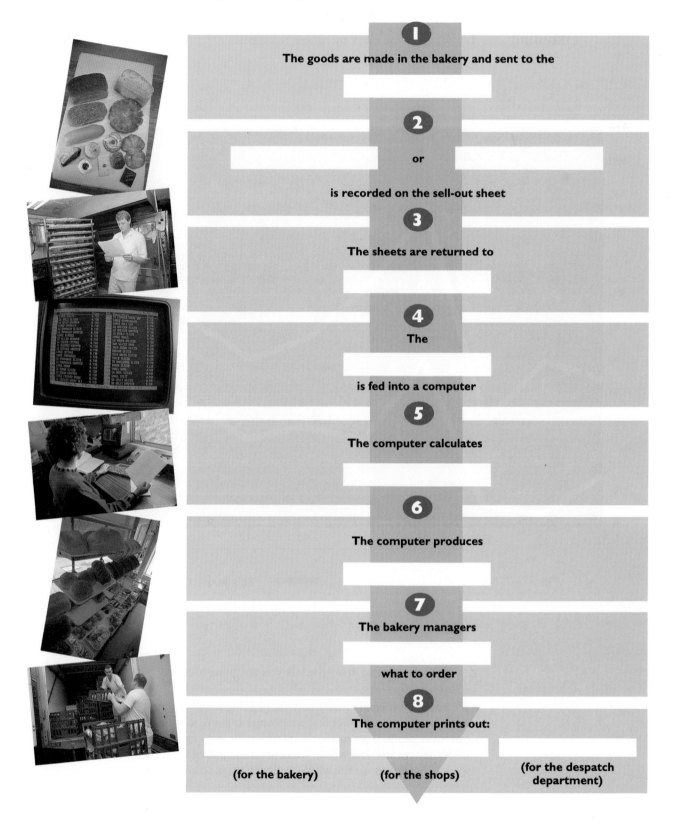

1

The goods are made in the bakery and sent to the

2

or

is recorded on the sell-out sheet

3

The sheets are returned to

4

The

is fed into a computer

5

The computer calculates

6

The computer produces

7

The bakery managers

what to order

8

The computer prints out:

(for the bakery)   (for the shops)   (for the despatch department)

Speaking   **1**   Draw a flow chart to describe a process in your workplace. You can choose any process you like. The ideas below may help you.

- developing a new product
- a manufacturing process
- a training process
- production planning
- ordering or buying goods
- an accounting process

2   Work in small groups. Take it in turns to give a short presentation to the group, describing the flow chart and explaining the process. Use these words to show the order of the steps in the process.

First of all . . .
After that . . .
Then . . .
Next . . .
Finally . . .

16

Negotiations

OBJECTIVE
to negotiate a business agreement

TASKS

to state and justify your position in a negotiation

to look for compromise solutions in conflict situations

to summarize a discussion and check what you've agreed

to read and discuss two articles on negotiating techniques

to negotiate the sale/purchase of a piece of machinery

PRESENTATION

1 You will hear three parts of a negotiation between managers in a multinational company. Listen to their conversation and complete the chart. The first person you will hear speaking is a manager from the company's head office. The second person is a manager from the company's foreign sales office.

	The subject of the discussion	What the head office wants	What the sales office wants	Do they reach a compromise?
Part 1	Sales Statistics			yes/no
Part 2				yes/no
Part 3				yes/no

142

2 Listen to Part 1 again and supply the missing words below. One word per space.

A We need better information about the market and (1) .... your help.

B What (2) ....

A (3) .... send us your sales statistics every week instead of every month.

B (4) .... difficult. It takes a long time to compile those statistics.

A I know but they're very important.

B If (5) .... you the statistics every week, (6) .... pay our costs?

A Could you be more specific?

B Would you pay for an extra day's secretarial help?

A It (7) .... be possible. One day, you say?

B Yes.

A OK. We (8) ....

3 Listen to Part 2 again and answer these questions.

1 How do they calculate the sales targets?
2 Why were last year's sales unusual?
3 How does the woman justify her argument? What does she say?

4

1 Listen to Part 3 again and complete this question:
   Could we go through .... ?

2 Which words are stressed in these sentences and why?

   You're going to send us your sales figures every week.
   And you're going to pay for four days' secretarial help each month.
   No. We agreed to pay for one day.

143

LANGUAGE WORK

Negotiating terms of sale

1 A customer and supplier are negotiating a contract of sale.

Put these sentences in the correct order. (The first and last sentences are numbered for you.)

☐	**Customer**	We didn't expect it to be so low.
☐	**Customer**	8 per cent.
1	**Customer**	What's the price?
☐	**Customer**	What discount could you offer?
☐	**Customer**	That's rather high.
☐	**Customer**	Supposing we agreed to a 5 per cent discount. Would you agree to a 60-day credit period?
☐	**Supplier**	I'm afraid that's not possible.
☐	**Supplier**	$65 per piece.
☐	**Supplier**	5 per cent.
☐	**Supplier**	It compares favourably with our competitors'. And on an order of this size we could offer a discount.
12	**Supplier**	No. Our terms of payment are 30 days. It's customary, I'm afraid.
☐	**Supplier**	What did you have in mind then?

2 Find phrases in the conversation that mean

1 How much are they?
2 That's expensive!
3 I'm surprised the discount isn't higher.
4 What discount did you expect?
5 You can't have 8 per cent.
6 If we said Yes to 5 per cent, would you give us 60 days' credit?
7 I'm sorry but we always do this.

Stating your position

1 Check that you understand the terms of sale below.

Price	$65 per piece
Credit period	30 days
Delivery time	8 weeks
Minimum order	500 pieces
Discount	5%
Cancellation penalty	50% for cancellation less than 4 weeks before delivery

The customer might complain about these terms.
The price is rather high.

What else might they say?
The credit period is . . .

Work with a partner. Take it in turns to be the customer and supplier.

Customer *What's the price?*
Supplier *It's $65 per piece.*
Customer *That's rather high.*
Supplier *It compares favourably with our competitors.*

These phrases will help the supplier to justify his or her position:

I'm afraid	*it's customary.*
	it's company policy.
	we always insist on this.

It compares favourably with our competitors.

2 Now take it in turns to query the terms.

Customer *We didn't expect the price to be so high.*
Supplier *What did you have in mind then?*
Customer *$60 a piece.*
Supplier *I'm afraid we couldn't accept that.*

3 The customer wants

- a long warranty period   (2 years)
- early delivery   (the end of next month)
- a penalty clause for late delivery   (−10% for each month of delay)
- a discount for bulk purchase   (−8% on orders over 1,000 pieces)
- an early settlement discount   (−2% for settlement within 14 days)
- good support documentation.   (a full set of manuals, free of charge)

Work with a partner again. Practise stating your position and asking for clarification.

Customer *We'd like a long warranty period.*
Supplier *Could you be more specific?*
Customer *Yes, we'd like a 2-year warranty period.*
Supplier *That's rather difficult but one year might be possible.*

Making compromises

1   A customer is buying some office furniture from a supplier. Look at the statements below and decide who could say them; the customer (C), the supplier (S), or either (C/S).

	C	S
1 We'd like you to increase the discount.		
2 We'd like you to pay in dollars.		
3 We'd like you to pay for delivery.		
4 We'd like you to pay for installation.		
5 We'd like you to reduce the price.		
6 We'd like you to accept a penalty clause for cancellation.		
7 We'd like you to accept a penalty clause for late delivery.		
8 We'd like you to pay by letter of credit.		
9 We'd like you to install the furniture over a weekend.		
10 We'd like you to let us use your offices as a showroom for our customers.		

2   Work with a partner. Take the part of the customer and supplier and suggest compromises.

Supplier   *We'd like you to pay in dollars.*
Customer   *If we paid in dollars, would you increase the discount?*
Supplier   *Yes, we could accept that./*
No, I'm afraid that's not possible.

3   Now go through the points again and check what you've agreed.

A   *Could we | go through that again?*
| check what we've agreed?
B   *Of course.*
A   *We're going to pay . . .*
B   *Yes, that's right./No. I thought we agreed . . .*

4   Work in small groups. Read the situations below and discuss the problems. Try to find compromise solutions.

1   A company has a machine that is 20 years old. It has broken down twice in the last four weeks and they have received two large repair bills from the machine manufacturer. They don't want to pay the second invoice for repair because they think the manufacturer didn't repair the machine properly the first time.

BEFORE YOU BEGIN, DECIDE WHO IS GOING TO REPRESENT THE COMPANY AND WHO IS GOING TO REPRESENT THE MACHINE MANUFACTURER.

2   A company is introducing a staff share-ownership scheme. Shares will be available to staff with eight or more years service at a price that is five per cent below their market value. The employees complain these conditions aren't attractive and they won't encourage them to buy company shares.

BEFORE YOU BEGIN, DECIDE WHO IS GOING TO REPRESENT THE EMPLOYEES AND WHO IS GOING TO REPRESENT THE MANAGEMENT.

3	A company's head office want all their sales representatives to come to a seven-day new product briefing. The regional sales offices think seven days is too long. They argue it will result in lower sales and they don't want to come.
	BEFORE YOU BEGIN, DECIDE WHO IS GOING TO REPRESENT THE HEAD OFFICE AND WHO IS GOING TO REPRESENT THE SALES STAFF.

4	A company wants its employees to take English lessons. The management and staff must decide who is going to pay for the courses and whether they should be in normal working time or outside office hours.
	BEFORE YOU BEGIN, DECIDE WHO IS GOING TO REPRESENT THE MANAGEMENT AND WHO IS GOING TO REPRESENT THE EMPLOYEES.

5	A company has found that their foreign agents often give customers wrong information about their products. The agents want the company to provide free sales literature printed in their language.
	BEFORE YOU BEGIN, DECIDE WHO IS GOING TO REPRESENT THE COMPANY AND WHO IS GOING TO REPRESENT THE AGENTS.

6	Employees at a steel manufacturing company want to change the structure of the working week. They want to work four ten-hour days (and have a three-day weekend) instead of working five eight-hour days. The management don't think this is a good idea.
	BEFORE YOU BEGIN, DECIDE WHO IS GOING TO REPRESENT THE EMPLOYEES AND WHO IS GOING TO REPRESENT THE MANAGEMENT.

Hypothesizing

We use *supposing* when we imagine hypothetical situations. Ask a colleague what they would do in the situations below.

1   Supposing your boss wanted you to spend your summer vacation taking a full-time English course. What would you do?

2   Supposing your company gave you a large sum of money to invest in your department. What would you spend it on?

3   Supposing someone offered you a job in Saudi Arabia at twice your present salary. Would you take the job?

4   Supposing the job were in the USA. What would you do?

5   Supposing you were made redundant. What would you do?

SKILLS WORK

Reading 1   **1**   Studies show that negotiations usually have four stages.

1   The beginning
2   The exchange of proposals
3   The problem-solving stage
4   The finish

Read these passages and decide which stage they are describing. Write in the number and title.

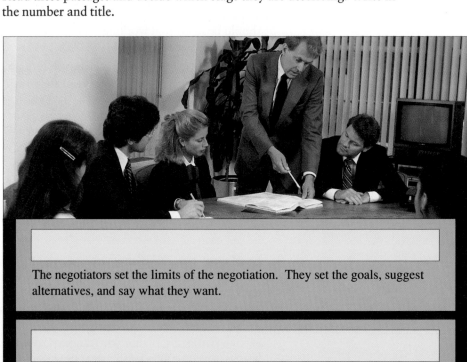

The negotiators set the limits of the negotiation. They set the goals, suggest alternatives, and say what they want.

At this stage the negotiators think about the future. Setting the agenda for the next meeting is the most important job.

At this stage the negotiators try to reduce the distance between what they want and what their partners want. They explain why the other side should change its position and make compromises. It's important to keep a positive atmosphere and find solutions.

The negotiators try to get to know each other so they can anticipate strategies and reactions. This is often a short informal stage in the West, but a longer and more formal stage in the East.

2 At which stage of a negotiation would you expect to hear the things below?

1 How long have you been working for Falworth Enterprises?
2 We can either send them by air or by sea.
3 How about meeting in Turin next time?
4 We think you should pay for the insurance because you're packing the goods.
5 We would like a two-year guarantee.
6 I'm sure we can solve this problem.
7 We need to discuss the product specifications.
8 We need to discuss the after-sales service next time we meet.
9 We'd pay for transport if you reduced your price.
10 I'm afraid we can't discuss reducing delivery times.
11 Have you ever been to Kobe before?
12 Supposing we paid in fourteen days. Would you give us an early settlement discount?

Speaking

Work in teams. You are going to negotiate the sale/purchase of a new machine. The buyers should use the information below and the suppliers should use the information on page 156.

You are all buyers. These are your targets for the negotiation. Go through the points with the other buyers before you begin and check that you understand them. You will have to compromise on most of these points if you want to make a deal.

	What you want	What you agree
Delivery time	6 weeks	
Warranty period	2 years	
Penalty clause	Late delivery penalty: −15% for each month of delay	
Training	Free training courses for the machine operators	
Price	$650,000	
Credit period	60 days	

Negotiate the deal with a supplier from the other team. Make a note of what you agree.

Compare your results with the other buyers. Who negotiated the best deal?

Reading 2   You are going to read an article that describes what good negotiators are like. Before you read it, read the statements below. In your opinion, are they true or false?

	T	F
• Good negotiators spend longer planning their strategy than other negotiators.		
• Good negotiators justify their arguments with lots of reasons.		

Now read the article and see if you agree with it.

What are good negotiators like?

Are they good planners, good talkers, good communicators? Neil Rackham and others of the Sheffield-based 5 Huthwaite Research group have done some research into the differences between 'average' and 'good' negotiators. They found negotiators with 10 a good track record and studied them in action. They compared them with another group of 'average' negotiators and found there was no 15 difference in the time the two groups spent on planning their strategy. However, there were some significant differences on other points.

The average negotiators 20 thought in terms of the present, but the good negotiators took a long-term view. They made lots of suggestions, and considered twice 25 the number of alternatives. The average negotiators set their objectives as single points - 'We hope to get $2.00', for example. 30

The good negotiators set their objectives in terms of a range, which they might formulate as 'We hope to get $2, but if we get $1.50 35 it'll be all right'.

The average negotiators tried to persuade by giving lots of reasons. They used a lot of different arguments. 40

The good negotiators didn't give many reasons. They just repeated the same ones. They also did more summarizing and reviewing, 45 checking they understood everything correctly.

1   Are these statements true (T) or false (F)?

	T	F

1 Neil Rackman is a negotiator.
2 Good negotiators spend more time planning their strategy
   before a negotiation.
3 Good negotiators argue, giving lots of reasons.
4 Good negotiators repeat the same arguments.
5 Good negotiators go back and check points again.

2   Use these words from the article in the sentences below.

average   (lines 7/8)   considered (line 25)   summarizing (lines 44/5)
significant (line 18)   persuade   (line 38)   reviewing   (line 45)
long-term   (line 23)

1   The contract is a bit out of date so we are .... it.
2   It won't show a profit for a year or two. It's a .... investment.
3   We spent hours talking to her but we couldn't .... her to
    change her mind.
4   He's not going to give the whole speech. He's just .... the
    main points.
5   We .... that idea at the last meeting but we decided against it.
6   There was a .... rise in the prices of raw materials last month.
7   It's not fast and it's not slow. It's just ....

3   *They have done some research.*
       They made lots of suggestions.

Some common expressions are often used with the verb *do* and others are
often used with the verb *make*.
       With a colleague, ask questions with *do* or *make*.

When did you last	*do*	*a telephone call?*
	make	*someone a favour?*
		a complaint in a shop or a restaurant?
		a difficult decision?
		some English homework?

4   Complete these sentences with the right form of *make* or *do*.

1   I'm afraid I've .... a mistake.
2   We haven't .... much progress.
3   That newspaper article .... a lot of damage to our reputation.
4   I'll phone round some suppliers and .... enquiries.
5   Have you .... business with them before?
6   Did we .... a profit on that line?
7   He .... me an offer I couldn't refuse.
8   What are we going to .... about this?
9   Can I .... a suggestion?
10 We need to .... a lot more research before we .... a decision.

ROLE-PLAY NOTES

Unit 1

Countries and Nationalities (p. 12)

2   Ask your partner questions to complete the table. Use the example below to help you.

A   *Where are the headquarters of Fiat?*
B   *In Italy.*
A   *So it's an Italian company.*

RANK BY SALES*	COMPANY	COUNTRY/NATIONALITY
8	Fiat	Italy/Italian
15	Samsung	
38	INI	Spain/Spanish
39	Petrobras	
46	Pemex	Mexico/Mexican
63	Petrofina	
88	Alcan Aluminium	Canada/Canadian
104	Broken Hill Proprietary	
129	Neste	Finland/Finnish
143	Koç Holding	

*Position in the *Fortune* list of the 500 biggest industrial corporations outside the US (1988)

Unit 2

Transferring Information (p. 17)

4   Dictate these messages to your partner.

Phone Vicki White between 2 and 4 p.m. tomorrow (0799 639154).

Send a quotation for 3,000 pieces, ref. no. 24/9987, to Ford Motor Company.

Fax invoice no. 24711 to head office.

Speaking 1 (p.20)

Call 1   Phone your partner and ask him/her to send you an up-to-date copy of their company's price list. Don't forget to give your name and address.

Call 2   Your partner phones you with a request. Say Yes and write down the details.

Speaking 2 (p. 23)

Telephone a foreign supplier and ask them to

- supply you with 40 lap-top computers – ALT 386SX
- quote you a price CIF
- translate the sales contract into English
- deliver in one month
- give you a two-year guarantee
- give you a 20% discount
- give you 60 days to pay.

Unit 3

Relocation (p. 29)

3 Your partner's company is thinking of relocating to Dukes Court. Look at the information below and answer his/her questions.

DUKES COURT
WOKING

Dukes Court is the finest office development in the country, and yet costs are half what you would expect to pay in the City of London. This magnificent 8 - storey building comprises 225,000 square feet of office space, equipped to the highest standards.

Consider just a few of the advantages of our prime location:

Rail - *BR station nearby with connections to Waterloo (27 minutes), and the South Coast.*
Road - *Close to the M25, and only 25 miles from London.*
Air - *Midway between Heathrow (20 minutes), and Gatwick (30 minutes).*
Parking - *space for over 400 cars.*

Consider also the benefits of:
600 telephone lines
21 lifts for passengers and goods
air conditioning
private tennis courts
......and more.

Call us for full details

Unit 4

Size and Dimension (p. 35)

3 You are the manager of a forwarding company. A customer phones to make enquiries. Use this information to answer their questions.

The dimensions of your trailers are:

Length – 12m
Width – 2m
Height – 2.5m

Their cubic capacity is 60m³.
The maximum load is 23,500 kgs.

You charge £1,350 to transport a full trailer-load to Rome. It takes 3–4 days.

Speaking 1 (p. 37)

Unit 5

Company History (p. 44)

4 You are the public relations officer of Facit – a Swedish office equipment company. A newspaper reporter is writing an article on your company. Use these notes on your company history to answer his/her questions.

1413	Facit starts trading in Sweden as a small copper mining company.
1889	Facit begins manufacturing furniture.
1928	Facit establishes its first subsidiary in Denmark.
1938	Facit acquires Halda typewriters. Facit introduces its products into the USA
1950	Facit establishes subsidiaries outside Europe in the USA and Brazil.
1956	Facit builds the first Swedish computer.
1969	Facit launches the 'Facit System 80' range of office furniture.
1973	Facit becomes a subsidiary of Electrolux.
1974	Facit sells the 'Facit Data Systems' business to Data Saab.
1979	Facit 2254 calculator becomes standard in Tokyo's largest bank.
1985	Facit launches its first laser printer.
1986	Facit sells the furniture division to Norwegian Design Funktion.
1988	Facit becomes a subsidiary of Entranor.

Unit 8

Fixing a Time (p. 73)

3 Here is your diary for next week. Your partner calls you.

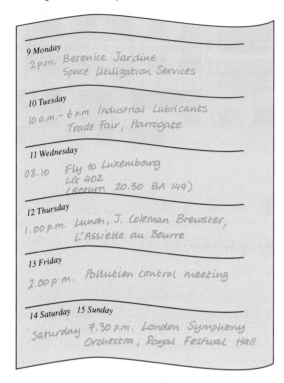

9 Monday
2 p.m. Berenice Jardine
Space Utilization Services

10 Tuesday
10 a.m. – 6 p.m Industrial Lubricants
Trade Fair, Harrogate

11 Wednesday
08.10 Fly to Luxembourg
LG 402
(return 20.30 BA 149)

12 Thursday
1.00 p.m. Lunch, J. Coleman Brewster,
L'Assiette au Beurre

13 Friday
2.00 p.m. Pollution control meeting

14 Saturday   15 Sunday
Saturday 7.30 p.m. London Symphony
Orchestra, Royal Festival Hall

Telex and E-mail (p. 76)

4 Group 2
Write another telex from Mr Nakagawa to Janet Jeffries changing his flight arrangements. (One person in the group should write and the others should dictate and check spellings.)

Your message

You regret you must change your plans.
You are now arriving on June 15th – not June 16th.
Flight number BAO18 – Terminal 4, Heathrow.
Your estimated time of arrival is 18.55.
You want Ms Jeffries to change the meeting with Data Link to June 16th.
You want her to advise you if she can't.
Say thank you.
Send your regards and sign the telex Nakagawa.

You will also receive a telex from the other group. Write a reply.

Speaking (p. 76)

1 You are expecting a visitor from your parent company for three days next week. The visitor wants to meet the people on this list. You contacted them to find out when they are free.

Mrs Carne	– Free any day before 12 a.m.
Mr Gandhi	– Free all day Tuesday, and Wednesday afternoon.
Miss Carley	– Free any time on Monday or Wednesday. Away all day on Tuesday.
Mr Barnes	– Away all day Monday. Free any time on Tuesday or Wednesday.
Ms Lyon	– Free 1–3 p.m. Tuesday and all day Wednesday.

The visitor phones you. Help to arrange his/her schedule. Pencil in the times.

21 Monday	9-10 am	
	10-11 am	
	11-12 am	
	12-1 pm	
	1-2 pm	
	2-3 pm	
	3-4 pm	
	4-5 pm	
22 Tuesday	9-10 am	
	10-11 am	
	11-12 am	
	12-1 pm	
	1-2 pm	
	2-3 pm	
	3-4 pm	
	4-5 pm	
23 Wednesday	9-10 am	
	10-11 am	
	11-12 am	
	12-1 pm	
	1-2 pm	
	2-3 pm	
	3-4 pm	
	4-5 pm	

2 The visitor calls you again with a problem. Help him/her to change the schedule. Change your notes.

Unit 9

Describing Graphs (p. 83)

Listen to your partner's description of the turnover of a company over a period of 12 months and complete the graph below.

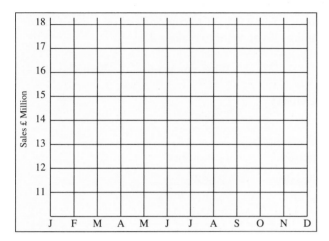

The graph below shows the energy costs of a company over a period of 12 months. Describe it to your partner.

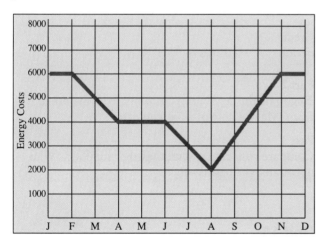

Unit 10

Targets (p. 92)

2 You have the sales figures for Rovocor and your partner has the sales figures for Mevacin. Exchange information and complete the table. Then decide who is 'Top Sales Person'.

		Last year	This year	Target	Difference (%)
Ms Catherine Ceretta	Mevacin				
	Rovocor	3,400	4,600	4,000	+15
Mr Philip Jacobsen	Mevacin				
	Rovocor	3,050	4,050	4,000	+1.25
Ms Annette Dubois	Mevacin				
	Rovocor	1,000	2,450	2,500	−2
Mr Peter Vogel	Mevacin				
	Rovocor	3,150	5,250	4,000	+31.25

Speaking: Investment Performance (p. 95)

You are a stockbroker. A client calls to find out how their shares have performed this week. Here is your client's portfolio. Tell him/her today's prices and give advice about what shares to buy more of and what shares to sell.

	Holding (No. of shares)	Last week's price (p)	Today's price (p)	Buy or sell?	Quantity
Nitro Chemicals	500	186	200		
Forsythe Bank	500	246	301		
Webb Communications	1,000	167	167		
Bespoke Tailoring	1,500	427	431		
Rose Computers	2,000	174	154		
Pharmedico Drugs	2,500	466	423		

This morning's headlines:

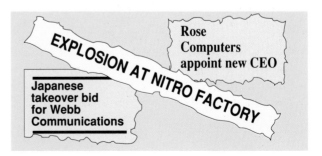

When you have finished, turn to page 156 for next week's share prices.

Unit 13

Reading: Cross-Cultural Contacts (p. 123)

Answers

1 You have to shake hands when you're coming or going in Germany, but in Britain you usually only shake hands when you meet someone for the first time.

2 You have to give your present in public in the Middle East to show it's not a bribe, but it's good manners to give your present in private in Asia.

3 You mustn't give cutlery in Latin America because it suggests that you want to cut off the relationship. You mustn't give food or drink in Saudi Arabia because it suggests you think your hosts aren't offering you enough to eat and drink. You mustn't give a clock in China because the Chinese word for *clock* is similar to the word for *funeral*.

4 'Come any time' means 'I want you to visit me' in India. If you don't suggest a time and arrange a visit immediately, an Indian will think you are refusing the invitation. But if an English person says 'Come any time', they will think you are bad-mannered if you start fixing a date.

5 Offices are usually closed on Fridays in Moslem countries.

6 Americans usually mean 'Yes' when they nod their heads. An English person probably just means 'I understand', and an Asian is just showing interest.

7 It's bad manners to discuss business at a social occasion in India.

8 In an English pub, you have to take your turn to buy a 'round' – a drink for everyone in your group.

Unit 16

Speaking (p. 149)

Part 1
You are all suppliers. These are your targets for the negotiation. Go through the points with the other suppliers before you begin and check you understand them. You will have to compromise on most of these points if you want to make a deal.

	What you want	What you agree
Delivery time	12 weeks	
Warranty period	12 months	
Penalty clause	Cancellation Penalty: 80% of total price	
Delivery and installation	Delivery charge: $1000. Installation charge: $750	
Price	$670,000	
Discount	5%	
Credit period	15 days	

Part 2
Negotiate the deal with a customer from the other team. Make a note of what you agree.

Part 3
Compare your results with the other suppliers. Who negotiated the best deal?

Unit 10

Speaking (p. 95)

Next week's share prices	
Nitro Chemicals	75
Forsythe Bank	276
Webb Communications	177
Bespoke Tailoring	435
Rose Computers	174
Pharmedico Drugs	483

Grammar Notes and Glossary

CONTENTS

GRAMMAR NOTES AND GLOSSARY

1 The Present Simple tense

EXAMPLES	USES	UNITS
Who **do** you **work** for? The training department **organizes** courses. He **lives** in Osaka.	Permanent or long-term situations	1 and 3
It **weighs** 2570 kgs. How long **does** it **take**? What **does** 'convenient' **mean**?	Facts	4
I usually **read** the *Financial Times*. How often **do** you **use** English at work?	Regular activities and routines	6
I **prefer** white wine. She **doesn't like** long meetings.	Feelings	6
I **don't agree**. How **do** you **feel** about this?	Opinions and states of mind	7
When **does** the London train **leave**? The board meeting **starts** at 3.30 p.m. It **doesn't finish** till 8.30.	Timetables and schedules	8

FORMATION	
• Add an *s* to the 3rd person singular form.	• Use *do* as a help verb to make negative forms.

I You We They	leave	at 8 a.m.
He She It	leaves	

I You We They	don't	leave at 8 a.m.
He She It	doesn't	

• Use *do* as a help verb to make question forms.
 	
Do | I | leave at 8 a.m.?
      you
      we
      they
Does | he
        she
        it
	• Use *do* as a help verb in short answers.
	
	Do you work for BICC?
	Yes, **I do.**
	
	Does she work for BICC too?
	No, she **doesn't.**

2 The Present Continuous tense

EXAMPLES	USES	UNITS
We're expanding our activities in China. **I'm waiting** for Miss Rowntree. **Who's calling** please?	Actions happening now	2
When **is** he **arriving**? **She's meeting** the CEO at 2 p.m. **Are** you **doing** anything special tonight?	Future plans and arrangements	8

FORMATION	
• Use the verb *be* and *-ing*. I am | (not) working today. You are He is She is It is We are They are • Don't forget to use contractions. I'm | I'm not You're | You aren't He's | He isn't She's | She isn't It's | It isn't We're | We aren't They're | They aren't	• Change the word order to form a question. Am I | working today? Are you Is he Is she Is it Are we Are they

3   The Past Simple tense

EXAMPLES	USE	UNITS
They shelved the project. I didn't have time to meet him. How long did you stay in Paris? What happened?	Finished past actions	5, 9, and 14

FORMATION	
• With regular verbs, add -ed to make the past simple form. Nissan opened the Yokohama plant in 1936. We launched our first laser printer in 1985. The meeting started late. • Irregular verbs have a special past form*. (to go) I went to a trade fair in Barcelona. (to rise) Inflation rose last month. * See page 168 for a table of common irregular verbs.	• Use *did* as a help verb to make negatives, questions, and short answers. The meeting didn't start on time. What time did you arrive? Did you go to the trade fair last month? Yes, I did. Did you? No, I didn't.

4   The Present Perfect tense

EXAMPLES	USES	UNITS
1 Past actions with present importance Kobe Steel has had excellent results this year. Home sales have increased. We've begun a joint venture project.	Giving news of recent events	10
The rationalization programme has led to better results this year. They haven't achieved the target.	Past actions with results in the present	10
She's worked in three different countries. Have you ever been self-employed? I've never taken time off work to do a training course.	Life experience	14
2 Actions that started in the past and are still continuing† He's been working for RKI Chemicals for 5 years. They've had a subsidiary in Puerto Rico since 1952. How long have they been in business? †See page 129 for more information on *for* and *since*, and page 127 for more information on the simple and continuous forms.	Unfinished actions	14

- Notice we use the past tense when a definite time is understood.

A We've opened a new factory in Roubaix.
B When did you do that?
A Last January.

A Have you ever been to China?
B Yes, I have. I visited Beijing in 1987.

A I've cancelled the order.
B Why did you do that?

- Americans sometimes use the simple past where the British use the present perfect.

US/English	Did you phone her yet?
British English	Have you phoned her yet?

FORMATION

Present perfect Simple

- Use *have* as a help verb in all forms.
Use it with the third part of the verb.

I You We They	have haven't	broken the machine.
He She It	has hasn't	

- Change the word order to form a question.

Have	I you we they	broken the machine?
Has	he she it	

- Use the help verb in short answers.

Have you spoken to the Legal department?
No, I **haven't**, but my colleague **has**.

Present perfect continuous

- Use *have* as a help verb in all forms.
Use it with *been* and *-ing*.

I You We They	have haven't	been working for an hour.
He She It	has hasn't	

- Change the word order to form a question.

Have	I you we they	been working for an hour?
Has	he she it	

- Use the help verb in short answers.

Has he been working here long?
No, he **hasn't**. Has she?
Yes, she **has**. She's been working here for 10 years.

5   Future time

EXAMPLES	VERB FORM	USES	UNITS
When **does** the London train **leave**? The Board meeting **starts** at 3.30 p.m.	The present simple tense	Timetables and schedules	8
When **is** he **arriving**? She's **meeting** the CEO at 2 p.m. **Are** you **doing** anything special tonight?	The present continuous tense	Future plans and arrangements	8
We're **going to** open a new sales office in Spain. Who **are** you **going to** invite to the meeting?	*going to* + stem	Intentions	7
Hold on. **I'll** get a pencil. She's busy. – Then **I'll** come back later.	*will* + stem	Instant decisions	2
We'll need a big hotel. How many people **will** work here? There **won't** be much space.	*will* + stem	Future facts and predictions	12

6   Modal verbs

Modal verbs are special help verbs. They add extra meaning to the main verb. Most modals have more than one use.

MODAL	EXAMPLES	USES	UNITS
can	**Can** I use your phone? **Can** you quote me a price CIF New York? Passengers **can** take a small bag onto the plane with them. I **can't** find my boarding card.	Permission Request Possibility Inability	2 2 13 13
could	**Could** I interrupt a moment? **Could** you speak up? We **could** ask for volunteers.	Permission Request Suggestion	2 2 7
may	**May** I borrow your car?	Permission	2
might	It **might** be possible to reduce the price.	Future possibility	16
will	How many people **will** work here? There **won't** be much space. **I'll** tell him to phone you back.	Future fact Prediction Promise	12 12 2

MODAL	EXAMPLES	USES	UNITS
would	**Would** you speak more slowly please? What **would** you like to drink? **Would** you like to come to a party? I'd love to. What time **would** suit you? **Would** you reduce the price, if we paid cash?	Requests Offers Invitations Suggestions	2 6 8 8 16
shall	**Shall** I call a taxi for you? **Shall** we ask for volunteers?	Offer Suggestion	6 7
should	I think we **should** teach the French sales staff English. It's a Spanish branch so we **should** employ Spanish nationals.	Recommending action Saying what is right or correct	7 7
must	Passengers **must** make sure their bags are clearly labelled. Passengers **mustn't** carry guns or explosives.	Obligation Prohibition	13 13

FORMATION

• Use the modal verb with the stem of the main verb. Don't add -s in the 3rd person singular.
 	
She **can** speak Russian and Chinese.
This product **will** sell well in the Far East.
 	
• Make a question by changing the word order.
 	
Could you call me back?
May I borrow your dictionary?
 	
• Make a negative by adding *not* to the modal verb.
 	
    can't   mustn't
    cannot   shouldn't
    couldn't wouldn't
	But be careful, there are some exceptions.
	
	1 *Will not* is very strong.
	  Won't is more common in spoken English.
	
	2 *Mightn't, mayn't* and *shan't* are unusual.
	
	• **Don't** use *do* as a help verb to make negatives and questions with modal verbs.
	• **Don't** use *to* after modal verbs.
	
	*Do you can swim? *I don't can swim.
	*We must to increase our productivity.
	
	THESE THREE ARE ALL WRONG

7   Comparatives and superlatives

EXAMPLES	USES	UNIT
This town has a higher rate of unemployment than the national average. The rates of pay are more competitive. English cars aren't as reliable as German cars.	Comparing two things	11
France has the best telecommunications system in Europe. Which country has the strongest economy?	Comparing three or more things	11

FORMATION	
Short adjectives	**Long adjectives**
• Add *-er* or *-est* to adjectives with one syllable.	• Use *more* or *most* with adjectives with two or more syllables.

high	higher	high**est**
cheap	cheap**er**	cheap**est**
big	big**ger**	big**gest**

Watch out for these three irregular forms.

good	better	best
bad	worse	worst
far	further	furthest

• Add *-er* or *-est* to adjectives with two syllables ending in *-y*.

easy	easi**er**	easi**est**

Long adjectives

expensive	**more** expensive	**most** expensive
convenient	**more** convenient	**most** convenient
competitive	**more** competitive	**most** competitive

Much

• Use *much* to make the comparative adjective stronger.

It's much more expensive.
The climate is much better in France than Scotland.

8 Conditionals

EXAMPLES	USES	UNIT
If there's a seat in economy, give me that.	instructions	13
If it's 11 a.m. in London, it's 8 p.m. in Tokyo.	facts	13
If she bought a discount ticket, she won't be able to change it.	future possibilities	13
If I were offered a job abroad, I'd take it.	hypothetical situations	16
If we agreed to 5 per cent, would you give us 60 days' credit?		

FORMATION
• In most conditional sentences, use the tenses that are natural and logical for the situation. But be careful. It's very unusual to use use *will* in the same clause as *if*. After *if* use a present tense to express a future idea.

If you buy 500, we'll give you a discount.

• In hypothetical situations, use a past form to express a future idea. This suggests something is less likely to happen.

If you bought 500, we'd give you a discount.

• You can put the *if* clause at the beginning or end of the sentence.

If I see him, I'll tell him.   If you paid cash, we'd give you a discount.
I'll tell him, if I see him.   We'd give you a discount, if you paid cash. |

9   The Passive Voice

EXAMPLES	USES	UNIT
The company's activities **are divided** into six business areas. It's **made** of paper. Nissan UK **was founded** in 1969.	to describe actions without saying who does them	3 4 5
The data **is fed** into the computer. The bumpers **are tested, packed,** and **loaded,** into lorries.	to describe processes	15

FORMATION
• Use the verb *be* as a help verb. Use the third part of the main verb (the past participle).

Then the | component **is** | **taken** to the factory floor.
        | components **are** |

10   Countable and uncountable nouns

English nouns are divided into two groups: countable nouns and uncountable (mass) nouns.*

Countables	Uncountables
• Countable nouns are singular or plural. machine machines job jobs	• Uncountable nouns are never plural. machinery work
• Countable nouns have singular or plural verb forms. That machine breaks down every week. Those machines break down every week. The job is very interesting. The jobs are very interesting.	• Uncountable nouns never have plural verb forms. That machinery breaks down every week. The work is very interesting.
• Singular nouns can have *a* or *an* in front of them. We need a new machine. It's an interesting job.	• Uncountable nouns never have *a* or *an* in front them. (*A* means *one* – and that's counting.) We need (some) new machinery. It's interesting work.
• Use *many* with countable nouns. How many new machines do we need? There aren't many jobs left to do.	• Use *much* with uncountable nouns. How much new machinery do we need? There isn't much work left to do.

* For more examples of countable and uncountable nouns see Units 6 and 12.

11 Numbers

CARDINALS AND ORDINALS

Cardinal		Ordinal		Cardinal		Ordinal	
1	one	1st	first	16	sixteen	16th	sixteenth
2	two	2nd	second	17	seventeen	17th	seventeenth
3	three	3rd	third	18	eighteen	18th	eighteenth
4	four	4th	fourth	19	nineteen	19th	nineteenth
5	five	5th	fifth	20	twenty	20th	twentieth
6	six	6th	sixth	21	twenty-one	21st	twenty-first
7	seven	7th	seventh	22	twenty-two	22nd	twenty-second
8	eight	8th	eighth	30	thirty	30th	thirtieth
9	nine	9th	ninth	40	forty	40th	fortieth
10	ten	10th	tenth	50	fifty	50th	fiftieth
11	eleven	11th	eleventh	60	sixty	60th	sixtieth
12	twelve	12th	twelth	70	seventy	70th	seventieth
13	thirteen	13th	thirteenth	80	eighty	80th	eightieth
14	fourteen	14th	fourteenth	90	ninety	90th	ninetieth
15	fifteen	15th	fifteenth	100	a hundred	100th	hundredth

0	*nought
100	a hundred
1,000	a thousand
1,000,000	a million
1,000,000,000	†a billion (US English)
1,000,000,000,000	†a billion (British English)

*0 is pronounced **nought** before a point and **oh** after a point in British English. It is pronounced **zero** is US English.

†In the past, US and British billions were not the same. But US billions are now often used by British companies and newspapers.

FRACTIONS

¼	⅓	½	⅘
a quarter	a third	a half	four fifths

DECIMALS

0.5	nought point five
0.25	nought point two five
10.06	ten point oh six
27.27	twenty-seven point two seven

- Write the decimal point sign as a dot, not a comma.
- Pronounce numbers individually after a decimal point.

166

12   Time

- A simple way to tell the time is to say the numbers.

10.20	*ten twenty*
11.15	*eleven fifteen*
4.45	*four forty-five*

- You can say the hours in two ways:

nine
nine o'clock

- But don't make this common mistake:

> * *nine-thirty o'clock*
> THIS IS WRONG

- If you need to be exact you can say : *ten a.m.*
  or   *ten in the morning*
  and   *ten p.m.*
  or   *ten at night.*

- You can also tell the time this way:

| one o'clock | ten past three | a quarter past four | half past five | twenty-five to six | a quarter to seven |

Days
Monday
Tuesday
Wednesday
Thursday
Friday
Saturday
Sunday

Months
January
February
March
April
May
June
July
August
September
October
November
December

Seasons
spring
summer
autumn
   (*US English*: fall)
winter

Years

Written	Spoken
1992	nineteen ninety-two
1066	ten sixty-six

Dates

	British English	US English
Spoken	The sixteenth of September September the sixteenth	Sixteenth September September sixteenth
Written	16(th) September 16/9/92	16 (th) September 9/16/92

Irregular Verbs

STEM	PAST TENSE	PAST PARTICIPLE	STEM	PAST TENSE	PAST PARTICIPLE
be	was/were	been	lose	lost	lost
become	became	become	make	made	made
begin	began	begun	mean	meant	meant
break	broke	broken	meet	met	met
bring	brought	brought	pay	paid	paid
build	built	built	put	put	put
buy	bought	bought	quit	quit	quit
catch	caught	caught	read	read	read
choose	chose	chosen	ride	rode	ridden
come	came	come	ring	rang	rung
cost	cost	cost	rise	rose	risen
cut	cut	cut	run	ran	run
deal	dealt	dealt	say	said	said
do	did	done	see	saw	seen
draw	drew	drawn	sell	sold	sold
drink	drank	drunk	send	sent	sent
drive	drove	driven	set	set	set
eat	ate	eaten	shake	shook	shaken
fall	fell	fallen	shoot	shot	shot
feed	fed	fed	show	showed	shown
feel	felt	felt	shut	shut	shut
fight	fought	fought	sing	sang	sung
find	found	found	sink	sank	sunk
fly	flew	flown	sit	sat	sat
forbid	forbade	forbidden	sleep	slept	slept
forget	forgot	forgotten	speak	spoke	spoken
freeze	froze	frozen	spend	spent	spent
get	got	got (*US*: gotten)	spread	spread	spread
give	gave	given	stand	stood	stood
go	went	gone	steal	stole	stolen
grow	grew	grown	stick	stuck	stuck
have	had	had	swim	swam	swum
hear	heard	heard	take	took	taken
hide	hid	hidden	teach	taught	taught
hit	hit	hit	tear	tore	torn
hold	held	held	tell	told	told
hurt	hurt	hurt	think	thought	thought
keep	kept	kept	throw	threw	thrown
know	knew	known	understand	understood	understood
lay	laid	laid	wear	wore	worn
lead	led	led	win	won	won
learn	learnt	learnt	withdraw	withdrew	withdrawn
leave	left	left	write	wrote	written
lend	lent	lent			
let	let	let			
lie	lay	lain			

Abbreviations

Abbreviation	Meaning	Example
ACC/ACCOM	Accommodation	PLS ARR HOTEL ACCOM IN CITY CENTRE
ADD	Addition/Additional	IN ADD PLS QUOTE FOR 200 PIECES
ADV	Advise	WILL TLX TOMORROW N ADV ETA
ARR	Arrive/Arriving	ARR LARNACA JUN 2
ARR/ARRNG	Arrange/Arrangement/Arranging	TNKS FOR ARRNG THE ITINERARY
APPROX	Approximate/Approximately	CASES WILL BE APPROX 1M × 2M × 2M
ASAP	As soon as possible	PLS CFM ASAP
ATTN	Attention	ATTN MR JORGE URIBE
BFOR	Before	PLS REPLY BFOR TUESDAY
CLD U	Could you	CLD U FWD DOCS TO MILAN OFFICE
CFM	Confirm	PLS CFM THESE PRICES
CHNG	Change	PLS CHNG HOTEL RESERVATION
DEL	Deliver/Delivery	DEL WAS 2 DAYS LATE
DEP	Departs/Departure	TRAIN DEP GARE DU NORD 14.25
DLY	Delay	RGT DLY IN REPLYING
DOCS	Documents	PLS FWD DOCS SOONEST
ETA	Estimated time of arrival	ETA IS 12.30
FAO	For the attention of	FAO MR ANDREW TIFFANY
FLGT	Flight	FLGT DEP 14.05
FWD	Forward (Send)	PLS FWD SAMPLES ASAP
INFO	Information	NEED MORE INFO BFOR WE CAN SUPPLY
INV	Invoice	RE YR INV NO 24016
L/C	Letter of Credit	SENDING L/C TO BARCLAYS BANK
LST	Last	RE OUR MTG LST WK
LTR	Letter	RE YR LTR DATED JAN 9
MAX	Maximum	3000 IS MAX WE CAN SUPPLY
MIN	Minimum	THIS IS OUR MIN PRICE
MTG	Meeting	PLS CANCEL MTG
N	And	PLS SEND 2 QUOTES – ONE CIF N ONE FOB
NO	Number	REF NO 29681
NXT	Next	SEE U NXT WK
OK	I agree/Agreement	CANNOT ORDER WITHOUT YOUR OK
OK?	Is this OK?	SEE U 3.30 FRIDAY, MILTON HOUSE, OK?
ORD	Order	REF YR ORD NO 846
OURLET	Our letter	RE OURLET DATED NOV 12
OURTELCON	Our telephone call	RE OURTELCON YESTERDAY
PLS	Please	PLS RPLY SOONEST
POSS	Possible	ARRG MTG FOR FRIDAY IF POSS
RE/REF	About/Reference	RE YR TLX DATED JAN 16
REC	Received	REC YOUR QUOTATION. MANY TNKS
RGDS	Regards	BEST REGARDS
RGRT	Regret	RGRT MUST CANCEL OUR MTG
RPLY	Reply	PLS RPLY BY RETURN TLX
SOONEST	As soon as possible	PLS RPLY SOONEST
THKS/TNKS	Thanks	TNKS FOR THE SAMPLES
TLX	Telex	PLS TLX BY RETURN
U	You	CLD U BOOK TICKETS
UR	Your	TNKS FOR UR HELP
VST	Visit	RE TRAINEES STUDY VST TO LISBON
WK	Week	ARR NXT WK
WLD U	Would you	WLD U POSTPONE APPOINTMENT
YR	Your	TNKS FOR YR HELP

Glossary

an **abbreviation** a short form. *Ad* is an abbreviation for *advertisement.*

absent away, not at work.

access *We have access to that information* = we can get it.

accommodation a place to stay (*please arrange hotel accommodation*).

to **achieve** to be successful, to reach an objective or goal.

to **acquire** to buy (Facit *acquired Halda Typewriters in 1938*).

an **advantage** a good point, a strength. Opposite = **a disadvantage.**

an **advertisement** Publicity designed to sell a product or service (*We put advertisements in the daily papers and sales increased by 20%*). Also **to advertise, advertising.** Abbreviations: **advert, ad.**

to **advise** to make helpful suggestions or recommendations: or, more formally, to inform (*Please advise us of your arrival date*). Also **advice.**

an **agenda** a list of things to discuss at a meeting.

an **agent** a person or company that represents the interests of another company in a market. Also **agency.**

an **alternative** a choice, a possible course of action, an option.

to **apply** to ask for something, officially and in writing (*I've applied for a US entry visa: he's applying for another job.*)

assets the things a company has or owns, including property, plant, equipment, stocks, money in the bank, and money owed by customers. Opposite = **liabilities.**

to **assist** to help.

to **attract** to create interest (*Good shop window displays attract customers*).

an **auditor** a person who examines a company's accounts, usually yearly, to see that they are in order.

average *The average of 4, 5, and 9 is six.*

to **award** to give a prize or certificate (*They awarded the Nobel Peace Prize to Lech Walesa in 1983*). Also **an award.**

an **axis** a fixed reference line for measuring on a graph (*vertical axis, horizontal axis.*)

a **barrel** a container for oil.

a **benefit** an advantage (*We offer a good salary and other benefits such as a company car*).

blue-chip profitable, offering a reliable investment and good prospects (*IBM is a blue-chip company*).

a **bonus** an extra sum of money paid to an employee (for example, a productivity bonus).

booming growing fast (*Business is booming: sales are up 80% on last year*).

a **border** a frontier, a line dividing two countries.

a **brand** a particular make of goods or their trademark.

to **break down** to stop working (*This machine has broken down. Can you repair it?*). Also **a breakdown.**

to **break even** to make neither profits nor losses on a business or product.

a **breakthrough** an important scientific, technological, or industrial discovery.

to **brew** to make beer.

to **bribe** to offer an illegal commission (*He obtained his competitors' plans by bribing a security guard*). Also **a bribe.**

to **brief** to inform (*Could you brief us on the progress of your project?*).

a **broker** a person who buys and sells things or (financial) services: **a stockbroker, an insurance broker.**

a **budget** an amount of money set aside for a special purpose (for example, *the advertising budget*). Also **to budget.**

a **bumper** a part of a car at front and back which protects it in small accidents (*US English:* **fender**).

to **cancel** to stop (*I'd like to cancel my appointment*).

capital a sum of money used to start a business. Also **capital expenditure** = money spent on buildings, equipment, etc.

cash money that is ready to spend, in notes and coins or (for a company) in a bank account.

cash flow the movement of cash in and out of a business.

to **catch** to take, and to be on time for, a plane, train, etc. (*I have to catch a train at 7 a.m.*): or to hear (*I didn't catch your name*). Opposite = **to miss.**

charity organizations that help poor or sick people (for example, the International Red Cross).

CIF (adjective/adverb) an export price including Cost, Insurance and Freight.

a **clause** a paragraph, section, or part of a legal contract.

colleagues people who work together.

a **competitor** another company operating in the same area of the market. Also **to compete: competition: competitive.**

to **compile** to collect and arrange information (*We're compiling statistics on regional sales costs*).

a **component** a part of a product.

to **compromise** to change a negotiating position in order to reach an agreement (*They wanted 10% and* *we wanted 6%, so we compromised and agreed to 8%).* Also a **compromise**.

to **confirm** to say something is true or correct (*Could you confirm that in writing?*). Also **confirmation**.

to **construct** to build. Also **construction**.

a **consumer** a person that buys goods or services. Also **consumption**.

to **contract work out** to pay another company to supply services (*We can stop employing security guards and contract the work out*).

convenient fitting in well with people's needs or plans, giving no problems (*Is 3.30 on Friday a convenient time?*).

core main, central, basic (for example, **core markets, core business**).

costs expenses, the money that has to be spent: *sales costs, energy costs.* Also **to cost** = to require a certain price to be paid (*This book costs £10.00: the price is £10.00): or* to estimate costs (*We need to cost the packaging. Ask for quotations from our suppliers*).

a **crash** a dramatic fall (for example, the Great Stock Market Crash of 1929).

a **crate** a box or container for goods.

a **currency** the money system of a country (*The currency of the USA is the dollar*).

a **curriculum vitae** a person's life history showing education and previous work experience (abbreviation: c.v.).

customary usual practice, normal (*It's customary to tip waiters 10% or 15%*).

to **cut** to reduce (for example, prices or budgets). Also **cuts, cutbacks**.

data information.

a **debt** money one has borrowed and must pay back: money one owes. Also **debtors** = people or companies that owe money.

to **defend** to argue in support of something: to protect against attack.

a **deficit** the amount by which a sum of money is too small (*We have £1m and we need £3m. That's a deficit of £2m*).

demand how much customers want goods or services. (*A rise in demand will result in a rise in supply or a rise in prices*).

to **demonstrate** to show something (for example, a machine) working. Also a **demonstration**.

dimensions the width, height, length, etc. of an object.

a **discount** a price reduction (*There's a 5% discount on large orders*).

to **dismiss** to stop employing someone, to sack or fire.

to **distribute** to send goods into a market. Also a **distributor: distribution**.

a **division** a major section of an organization.

a **document** an official paper.

a **donation** an amount of money given away (*We made a small donation to charity*).

due expected (*Payment is due at the end of the month*): or because of (*The increase in sales was due to the large orders from Japan*).

duty tax paid when importing goods.

to **earn** to get money, by working or as a return on an investment. Also **earnings** = returns, profits on an investment.

economical saving money (*Get a smaller car. It's more economical*).

an **economy** a country's finances, trade and industry (*The Soviet economy entered a crisis in the late 1980s*). Also **economic**.

EDP Electronic Data Processing.

efficient working well and quickly, producing a good result in the minimum time. Also **efficiency**.

to **employ** to give work to someone (*This factory employs 150 people*). Also **employer** (the company): **employee** (the worker): **employment** and **unemployment**.

to **enclose** to put something in an envelope with a letter. Also **enclosed**.

engaged busy (on the telephone).

enhanced made better, improved.

to **enquire** to ask questions to get information. Also **enquiry**.

to **establish** to set up, to begin (*We established our first Asian subsidiary in Singapore last year*): or to find out, to discover (*to establish the facts*).

to **exceed** to be more than, to go above (*temperatures in Britain don't often exceed 30 degrees Celsius*).

expenditure money spent on something.

exports goods sold abroad. Also **to export**.

facilities rooms, equipment or services.

a **factory** a building where goods are manufactured.

a **fault** a defect or mistake.

a **feasibility study** a study to see if something is possible, or will work, or will be profitable.

to **fire** to sack, to dismiss, to stop employing someone.

a **fleet** a group of ships, cars or lorries (*CGM has 77 ships in their fleet*).

to **focus** to concentrate (*We focused our attention on the East European market*).

a **forwarding company** a company in the business of transporting goods.

a **fraud** a crime where money is obtained by lying, or by hiding the truth.

global worldwide, covering the whole world.

grateful thankful (*I'd be grateful if you could send me . . .*).

gross before anything is taken away: for example, **gross profits** = profits before tax. Opposite **net**.

a **guarantee** a promise accepting responsibility for something. Also **to guarantee** (*We can guarantee delivery in seven days*).

headquarters the main office of a company. The **headquarters** of BMW are in Munich.

a **holding company** a parent company, a company controlling shares in a subsidiary.

imports goods bought from abroad. Also **to import**.

to **improve** to make better: to get better. Also **improvement**.

an **incentive** something (for example money) that encourages people to do things.

inflation the general increase in the price of goods and services.

to **insist** to refuse to accept an alternative or a compromise.

to **install** to put in place (*We'd have to install the new machine before we can start production*).

interest money charged (for example, by a bank) for borrowing money.

inventory stocks of goods.

to **invest** to spend money in order to make a profit, for example by buying machinery for a factory, or shares in a company. Also **investment** = the activity of investing *or* the money that is invested.

an **invoice** a list of goods sold with a request for payment. Also **to invoice**.

an **item** a subject, a thing (*An item on the agenda*).

an **itinerary** a plan for a visit or journey, showing places, dates, times, and people to see.

a **joint venture** a co-operative operation between two companies, sharing expertise, resources, etc.

to **justify** to show that something is fair or reasonable. Also **justification**.

labour force staff, employees, the people employed or who can be employed.

to **launch** to introduce a product to a market.

leading in the first position, in front of the competition (*IBM is the world's leading computer firm.*)

to **lease** to rent or hire. Also **a lease** = the written agreement to lease.

a **letter of credit** a bank document arranging payment for goods. Synonym = a **draft.**

liabilities debts, money a company owes to suppliers, shareholders, banks, etc.

a **lift** a machine for moving from one floor of a building to another (*US English:* **elevator**): *or* free transport (*I'll give you a lift to the office*).

links connections (*Holland has excellent transport links with Europe*).

a **list** names, items, etc., written or printed (*Can I see the wine list?*).

a **load** *What's this lorry's maximum load?* = the maximum it can carry. Also **to load** = to put goods onto a lorry, train, ship, plane, etc.: **a loading bay** = the place where lorries are loaded.

a **loan** a sum of money borrowed from a bank.

located positioned, placed, situated (*The United Nations is located in New York*). Also **location.**

a **loss** the money lost by a business: total sales minus total costs (if this figure is negative). Also **a profit and loss account** = a company's trading figures, usually for one-year period.

mail order buying or selling goods by post.

mains services supplies of gas, electricity, water, etc.

to **maintain** to keep in good working order. Also **maintenance.**

to **manage** to control and organize a business. Also **management**, and **a manager.**

to **manufacture** to produce, in large quantities with machinery.

a **market** a geographical area, or a section of the population, where you can sell products.

mass production production in large quantities, on a large scale.

a **merchant bank** A bank specializing in commercial loans and finance for industry.

to **merge** To join together (usually two companies). (*Renault and Volvo merged in 1990*). Also **a merger.**

a **mile** 1.6 kilometres.

to **modify** to change, to alter. Also **modification.**

a **mortgage** a loan used to buy a house or property.

a **multinational** a company with operations in many countries.

to **negotiate** to bargain, to discuss a business deal or contract, to reach an agreement by discussion. Also **(a) negotiation.**

net after everything is taken away. For example, **net profit** = profit after tax and other deductions. Opposite = **gross.**

an **objective** a target or goal.

an **overdraft** a negative sum in a bank account.

to **owe** to be in debt: (*We borrowed £5m and we've paid back £3m, so we still owe £2m*).

to **own** to possess, to have something as one's property. Also **owner, ownership.**

to **pack** to put in boxes or containers ready for sale. Also **a pack** = the box a product is sold in: **packaging** = the container or materials that provide protection for a product to be transported.

to **pay** to give money in return for goods and services. Also **payment.**

a **penalty** a punishment for breaking a contract.

personnel employees, staff. Also the section of a company dealing with staff matters such as recruitment or training.

(a) **plant** a factory: *or* the machinery that is in a factory.

a **policy** a plan of action, or usual rules for doing things (*It's our policy to ask for payment within 30 days*).

a **pool** a common supply of things. For example, a **car pool** = where cars are available when people need them.

to **postpone** to delay, to put something off to a later date.

premises buildings, offices, property.

to **produce** to make or manufacture. Also a **product** = the thing you produce: a **product manager** = the person responsible for the production and marketing of a product: **production** = the activity of producing: **productivity** = the efficiency of production.

a **profit** the money made by a business: total sales minus total costs (if this figure is positive). Also **profitable** = making a profit: **a profit and loss account** = a company's trading figures, usually for a one-year period.

a **project** a plan, a scheme of work.

to **promote** to give someone a more important job: *or* to organize an advertising event. Also **promotion**.

to **provide** to offer, to give (*We provide a 24-hour emergency service*).

public relations the work of distributing information to give a good impression of an organization.

to **purchase** to buy.

qualified having the right education, diplomas, and experience for a job. Also **a qualification**.

quality How good or bad something is (*A Rolls-Royce is expensive because of its very high quality*).

quarterly every three months (*a quarterly report*).

to **quote** to give an estimate for the cost products or services. Also **a quotation**.

a **range** a group of products sold by one company.

a **rate** how fast something happens (*the rate of inflation*) or the level of something (*interest rates, exchange rates*, etc.).

a **receipt** a document showing you have paid for something.

reception a meeting place in a hotel or company: *or* a party where you can meet people. Also **a receptionist** = the person who receives visitors when they enter a company or hotel: **a reception desk** = the place where a receptionist works.

to **recommend** to suggest, to speak well of someone or something (*Can you recommend a good hotel?*). Also **a recommendation**.

to **recover** to get better after a difficult period. Also **recovery**.

to **recruit** to employ or take on new staff. Also **recruitment**.

redundant no longer needed, dismissed, without work. Also **redundancy**.

reference With **reference to . . .** (in a letter) = concerning, about. Also **a reference** = a recommendation from an employer.

to **refund** to pay back money spent (*If you are not satisfied with this product, send it back within 30 days and we will refund you*).

refurbished completely redecorated.

to **register** to give your name when you arrive somewhere (*He registered with the receptionist and went into the conference*).

to **reject** to say No to a proposal, idea, offer, etc.

reliable consistently good in quality or performance or work.

to **rent** to hire, to borrow something in return for money. Also **rent** = the money paid to rent something.

a **reservation** a booking (*You have a reservation at the Hilton for 3 nights from Sunday*). Also **to reserve**.

to **resign** to give up or leave a job.

a **retail outlet** a place where goods are sold to the public, for example a shop or supermarket. Also **retailing** = selling to the public: a **retailer** = a person or company that sells to the public: the **retail price index** = an index to measure inflation.

retained kept, saved (*The retained profit is added to the company's reserves*).

to **retire** to stop working at the end of a career, usually between the ages of 55 and 65.

a **return** profit, earnings on an investment.

to **review** to re-examine, to consider in order to improve (*We're reviewing our distribution arrangements*).

to **sack** to dismiss, to fire, to stop employing someone.

a **salary** a monthly payment for doing a job.

a **sales prospect** a possible future customer.

a **sales representative** a person in a company who sells products to distributors or customers in a certain market (abbreviation: a **sales rep**).

a **schedule** a timetable. Also **to schedule** (*Shall we schedule a meeting for Thursday?*).

to **set up** to begin or establish something (*Henry Ford set up his first business in 1899*).

(a)**share** a part, a fraction (*We have increased our market share by 2%*): a part of a company (*We now have 51% of the shares, so we control the company*). Also a **shareholder** = a person who owns shares.

to **shelve** to postpone, to delay, to stop (*We had very little money left, so we had to shelve the project*).

to **ship** to transport, by sea or air. Also **a shipment** = the goods being transported.

to **short-list** to reduce a large number of alternatives to a short list of perhaps six or less, (for example, applicants for a job, sites for a new factory).

a **shortage** a situation where there is not enough of something (*There is a constant shortage of water in the Sahara*).

to **sign** to write one's name on a document. Also **a signature**.

single not married (*He's single*): for one person (*I'd like a single room*): in one direction only, one-way (*I'd like a single ticket*).

skilled trained, experienced (*It's a difficult operation: we'll need skilled workers*).

sound secure, certain, steady (*a sound investment*).

specifications details and instructions describing design and materials (*product specifications: building specifications*).

staff the people who work for a company, its personnel, its employees.

a **stake** a number of shares in a company.

stock goods in storage waiting to be sold: components in storage waiting for use in manufacturing.

a **strategy** a major plan or policy (*How are we going to achieve this objective? What's our strategy?*). Also **strategic**.

a **strength** a strong point.

a **strike** the organized stopping of work by employees as a result of a disagreement (*The workers went on strike for higher wages*).

a **subsidiary** a company that is controlled by another company (*NV Philips owns over 50% of Philips UK: so Philips UK is a subsidiary of NV Philips*).

a **suite** a group of rooms in a building.

to **supply** to provide customers with goods. Also a

supplier = a person or company that supplies goods.

support help, assistance.

to **take over** to take control of a company by buying a large number of its shares. Also **a takeover**.

a **target** a result one wants, a goal or objective.

a **task** a job, a piece of work.

tax money that a person or company pays to the government.

a **track record** a history of past success or failure.

trade buying and selling. Also **a trade balance** = the difference in value between a country's imports and exports.

to **transfer** to move from one place to another (*We've transferred the Finance department to the new offices: Could you transfer me to Peter Keller in the Finance Department?*)

a **trend** a pattern of change, a general movement (*a downward trend in the market*, etc.).

turnover the total sales of a company. Also **staff turnover** = the rate of staff leaving and joining a company.

a **TV commercial** an advertisement on television.

urgent needing immediate attention.

a **volunteer** a person who asks or offers to do a job (*I need three volunteers to work late tonight*).

a **wage** a weekly payment for doing a job, usually paid to manual workers.

a **warehouse** a large building where goods are stored.

a **warranty** a legal guarantee, a promise to repair or replace a product if it is not satisfactory.

to **win** to come first, to beat competitors.

Oxford University Press
Walton Street, Oxford OX2 6DP

Oxford New York Toronto Madrid Delhi
Bombay Calcutta Madras Karachi Kuala Lumpur
Singapore Hong Kong Tokyo Nairobi
Dar es Salaam Cape Town Melbourne Auckland
and associated companies in
Berlin Ibadan

OXFORD and OXFORD ENGLISH are trade marks
of Oxford University Press

ISBN 0 19 451384 X
© Oxford University Press 1991
First published 1991
Fourth impression 1992

Set by Pentacor plc
Printed in Hong Kong

Illustrations by:
Martin Cox, Jane Hughes, Margaret Jones, Alex
McOwan, Nigel Paige, Donald Thomas, David Loftus.

*The publishers would like to thank the following for
their permission to reproduce photographs:*
AB Tetra Pak; AMP of Great Britain Ltd.; Amstrad
plc/Michael Joyce; Asda; Beazer plc; BICC plc; Boral
(UK) Ltd.; The British Petroleum Company plc;
J Allan Cash; Martyn Chillmaid; Fine Art
Developments Ltd. (Premiere); Robert Harding Picture
Library; Nigel Hawkins Associates; Kobe Steel Europe
Ltd.; Lex Vehicle Leasing Ltd.; MEPC plc; Metropole
Hotels; Next; Nissan UK Ltd.; Nissan Motor Company
Ltd.; Peugeot Talbot Motor Company Ltd.; Philips;
Science Photo Library; Nicholas Sergeant; Derek
Stirling; Telegraph Colour Library; Zefa.

Location photography by Rob Judges, with thanks to
Ideal Bakeries Ltd.

Designed by Shireen Nathoo

Acknowledgements
*The author and publishers would like to thank the
following for permission to reproduce copyright
material:*

Associated Newspapers plc; BICC plc; Boral (UK) Ltd.;
The British Petroleum Company plc; Daily Mail; The
Economist Newspaper Ltd.; Facit Ltd.; Grid Publishing
Inc. (for permission to reproduce part of *International
Business Blunders* , by Ricks, Fu, and Arpan); House of
Stirling (Direct Mail) Ltd.; Innovations (Mail Order)
Ltd.; Kobe Steel Europe Ltd.; Lex Van Contracts;
Management Publications Ltd.; MEFC Investments;
Metropole Hotels (Holdings) Ltd.; Nederlandse Philips
Bedrijven BV; Geo. Ort Ltd.; The Society of
Management Accountants of Canada (for permission
to adapt an article appearing in *CMA* by J.M. Hewer);
Derek Stirling and John Swire & Sons Ltd.; Tetra Pak
Ltd.; Time Inc. Magazines; Trans World Airlines Inc.;
Venture Marketing Ltd.

The author would like to thank the many friends,
relatives, colleagues, and acquaintances who have
helped in writing this book. Special thanks to Emma
Tanner and Liz Lyon for their help in the planning
stages, Roger Carter for his help at the end, and to Sue
Osborne for typing the manuscript. Many thanks also
to Suren Advani, Geoff White, David Morris, Nigel
Newbrook, Peter Ort, and Bob and Kim Shaw for
allowing me to tape them in action. Last but not least,
my warmest thanks to EF Language Schools and all
the staff at EF Private Study Centre Cambridge, for
their help in piloting these materials. Their advice and
suggestions were invaluable.